The Accidental Housewife

The Accidental HOUSEWIFE

HOW TO OVERCOME
HOUSEKEEPING HYSTERIA
ONE TASK AT A TIME

Julie Edelman

BALLANTINE BOOKS / NEW YORK

Published in the United States by Ballantine Books, an imprint of The Random House Publishing Group, a division of Random House, Inc., New York.

BALLANTINE and colophon are registered trademarks of Random House, Inc.

The Accidental Housewife, Housewife Intelligence Quotient, and HI Q are trademarks of Carpe Diem Communications, Inc.

All photographic caricatures in this work are reproduced courtesy of RubberBall Productions, copyright © RubberBall Productions.

LIBRARY OF CONGRESS CATALOGING-IN-PUBLICATION DATA
Edelman, Julie.

The accidental housewife : how to overcome housekeeping hysteria one task at a time / by Julie Edelman.
p. cm.
ISBN 0-345-49043-6 (pbk. : alk. paper)
1. Housekeeping. 2. House cleaning. 3. Home economics. I. Title.
TX301.E34 2006
640—dc22   2005057185

Printed in the United States of America

www.ballantinebooks.com

2 4 6 8 9 7 5 3 1

Book design by Casey Hampton

I've been baking bread and looking after the baby ... (With what secret projects going on in the basement? asks Playboy*) ... That's like what everyone else who has asked me that question over the last few years says. "But what else have you been doing?" To which I say, "Are you kidding?" Because bread and babies, as every housewife knows, is a full-time job. After I made the loaves, I felt like I had conquered something. But as I watched the bread being eaten, I thought, well, Jesus, don't I get a gold record or knighted or nothing?*

—JOHN LENNON, from *John Lennon and Yoko Ono on Love, Sex, Money, Fame, and All About the Beatles* (*Playboy*, January 1981)

Acknowledgments

Having never done this before, I will err on the side of thanking almost everyone I've ever known—with a few exceptions such as my mother's obstetrician—who have helped me joyfully come out of the broom closet and admit to being an accidental housewife, and have made this book a reality. Mia cuppas, to anyone I've forgotten. If I've done so, and if you'll pardon the expression, it is truly by accident.

The first folks I want to thank are the two who unintentionally made me realize that I was an accidental housewife: Bill Geddie and Alexandra (Dusty) Cohen, who thought my original name for a TV series about housewifely stuff was boring and thus *The Accidental Housewife* was born. Next, is my incredibly supportive literary agent extraordinaire, Jenny Bent, who believed in my book from the get-go, guided me seamlessly through the journey, and made sure it got into all the right hands. Which leads me to my fab and ego building editor Caroline Sutton, whose gentle, reassuring ways got me through a few "feng shui" meltdowns, and who made making deadlines painless, and writing this a wonderful experience. As did Christina Duffy, Caroline's ace assistant, who was always eager to provide any assistance needed or incorporate last-minute edits I phoned in.

Mucho kudos and thanks to the savvy marketing and publicity folk: Kim Hovey, Tom Perry, Carol Schneider, Lisa "fellow Dukee" Barnes, Christine Cabello, and all those who worked with them for getting this book and me to all the right people and places in record time; and to the creative team, led by Gene Mydlowski, who did an amazing job making me look good with broken ribs and interpreting my accidental housewifely vision along with Barbara Bachman's interior design group; Patrick Wilson for all his tweaks; and the incredibly talented designer of the logo, Supon, who brought it all together.

And, of course, big hugs to my husband and my son whom I love more than words can express for unselfishly playing golf every weekend so I could be left alone to write—and, who can't wait until I start my next book for the same reason!

I also want to thank the wonderful Bobbi Brown for her eagerness to share her words of wisdom without hesitation; gracias to my dear friends Geoffrey Menin and Kim Schefler, who always cheer me on and remind me that patience is a "good thing"; Kate Sullivan, my trusty research assistant, Marcia Parris for her family's "accidental insights," Seth Siegel for his etymology lessons; Liz (whom everyone else calls Elizabeth!) for making me look terrific even when I feel like the pix of the person introducing Task #1; my best bud and sister-in-law Gayle for being there when I needed to vent; and the mahvelous Marsha Tauber for giving me my first pair of wonderfully fashionable and functional pink rubber gloves that are just *so* me and for introducing me to our super-talented LA pal, Kim!

AND, LASTLY BUT NOT LEASTLY, a heart-felt thank you to all of my fellow accidental housewives who inspire me every day to discover fun, hassle-free ways to overcome our household hysteria one task at a time.

Ok not lastly ... Thanks to my loving mother, father, and yes, my mom's obstetrician, too, for bringing me into this wonderfully accidental world!

Contents

INTRODUCTION

Welcome to Our World!

Once upon a time, in a society far, far away, before lattes, TiVo, Roombas, nannies, and e-mail ruled the world, there lived a species of 1950s' women known as "housewives." These housewives lived in a time of freshly delivered milk, scheduled dinner around the televised broadcasts of *I Love Lucy* and *The Honeymooners,* danced nonchalantly through their household duties, washed stinky diapers, and catered to their hardworking husbands' every need. In sum, and to quote a 1955 *Housekeeping Monthly* article called "How to Be a Good Wife," the housewife's goal was to "try to make sure your home is a place of peace, order and tranquillity where your husband can renew himself in body and spirit." And so it was ... the 1950s' housewife embraced her role with pride, certainty, and held the world joyfully in the palm of her hand with duster in tow.

That was then. . . . This is now.

Today's housewife is a new and *very* different species. We hold the world in our Palm, but it is an electronic one. And we'd rather be doing lunch than doing dishes.

Then, life happens. Some of us get married, some of us move in with a significant other, some have children, buy a home, and find that suddenly, without warning, we've become a housewife! Fear and loathing set in, as does a new, unfamiliar source of stress disguised in piles of dirty laundry, endless dust bunnies, poop, and juggling schedules. And just when we thought it couldn't get any worse, we accidentally sit on the toilet bowl with the seat up after our beloved "males" have dribbled all over it! Not even Martha Stewart could turn this scenario into a "good thing." Yet a good thing for today's housewife *is* how to make the imperfect perfect for our lifestyle, ability, and most of all our level of interest in mastering our domain.

That is why I have written this book. After years of struggling to perfect my imperfections, I can now joyfully come out of the broom closet and tell all that I am not a domestic goddess nor a perfect mother (sorry, Mom!). I am an accidental housewife who has been in denial. And I have discovered that I am not alone. I am one of millions who are connected not by our gender but by our household responsibilities and activities. We are young and old, male and female, straight and gay, married and single, with and without children. We are the new species of housewife.

So, fellow accidental housewives, unite! This is our time to come out of the broom closet and celebrate our housewifely imperfections, fear, and loathing. It is our time to embrace our accidental style with a smile and for you to use, abuse, or be amused by what lies within this sanity-saving book. Now, pour your favorite libation and get ready to overcome your housekeeping hysteria one task at a time!

My Accidental Housewifely Author Reminders and Precautions

As you read through this book please keep in mind a few things:

- This is not a literary masterpiece like *War and Peace* (or at least not in the classic Tolstoy sense). It is a fun and hopefully useful guide to get you through the mundane tasks of housekeeping. If you choose instead to use it for bathroom reading, it will be equally as entertaining.
- I and others have tested, retested, and gathered the shortcuts and tips in this book from a variety of personal, everyday, and fellow accidental-housewife experiences and sources, but I cannot guarantee that each member of our species will enjoy the same results from the shortcuts and tips tried. I like to think of it as instructions we read on recipes that state "cooking times vary depending upon your oven." Results in our case will vary according to our individual interest, resolve, and time dedicated to the task.
- Though I have worked with some of the companies mentioned

in this book, all products, websites, services, organizations, expert advice, and anything else that starts with a capital letter are included in here *solely* because they fulfilled one or more of the following criteria:

- Ease to find in the store, online, or wherever
- Personal trial, error, and familiarity
- Recommendation by friends and colleagues
- They're my accidental housewifely faves.

Furthermore, since this book will be part of your everyday reading for years to come, prices and availability of products and services mentioned may vary by where you live, if something has been discontinued or outlawed, or if it's been replaced by a new improved version. In particular, please keep in mind that information on websites change almost as often as the weather does, so I can't vouch for the accuracy or content of anything that appears on the Internet or on websites other than my own. (And just for the record, my publisher has nothing to do with any of the websites I mention—not even mine—so my advice is to use your common sense and err on the side of caution when dealing with cyberspace!)

- Lastly all the household, exercise, beauty, and grooming activities suggested are shared with the understanding that some are in here for a yuk and others will require you to do them according to your individual ability and personal tolerance level. As any accidental housewife knows, *accidents happen*—so be careful!

Task #1
CLEANING

**WHO SAID CLEANLINESS IS
NEXT TO GODLINESS?**

I t seems like *OH-MY-GOD*-liness would probably be a more accurate statement. After all, cleaning brings us into a world filled with *ungodly* and varying amounts of dust, dirt, and doo-doo. Surely not the world we dreamed of when we imagined life as an adult. But facts are facts and cleaning is one of the main tasks of our accidental housewifely life. So how do we balance preaccidental hopes and dreams with our current reality? By having the right tools at hand and knowing how to maximize their results with the minimum amount of effort. These tools include everything from common household stuff you probably never dreamed could be used for cleaning, to a huge array of disposable products, to robotic help and help that lives and breathes, whom I lovingly refer to as D.A.s—Domestic Assistants. It is a combination of these tools, some simple know-how, and the right music that will make this ungodly task easier and enable you to preserve your sanity, your shape, your hair, and your hands. So in the words of one of my favorite singing groups, The Black-Eyed Peas, *"Let's Get It Started"*!

THE ACCIDENTAL HOUSEWIFE'S CLEANING BASICS

Man is made for something better than disturbing dirt.

—OSCAR WILDE

As you may have guessed, I'm not going to bog you down with the traditional list of household cleaning must-haves and tips that nonaccidental cleaning gurus can give you *unless* they complement our way of doing things. What I am going to do is share some useful shortcuts and stuff that I have found will make your home look clean enough to keep health inspectors away and enable you to pass the white-glove test—so long as you clean before company arrives!

Numero Uno Cleaning Rule:
Focus First on High-Traffic, High-Visibility Areas

As you ponder this rule, there are three things to keep in mind:

1. This is The Cosmetic Clean, which will achieve an acceptable, surface-clean home.
2. This is *not* The Big Clean, which you or someone else will have to do sometime this century.
3. What The Cosmetic Clean definition of high-traffic, high-visibility areas is: High-traffic, high-visibility areas generally include bathrooms, kitchens, and major living spaces that you use most often and are likely to be seen by visitors. They do not include your bedroom, which, if your life is as fatiguing as mine, sadly sees little activity other than side-to-side tossing and turning. For those of you who are more active, such as newlyweds, newly involved, or oversexed individuals, you can easily do The Cosmetic Clean in your bedroom by turning your covers down

daily, fluffing your pillows, spraying your room with air freshener regularly, throwing your laundry under your bed or in a laundry basket, and washing your sheets at least once a week.

As for your attention to *non*-high-traffic, high-visibility areas— that will depend upon your comfort level with dirt and the number of people living in your household. The good news is that The Cosmetic Clean can keep your home decent for a week or two, though bathrooms should be done weekly. The not-so-good news is eventually you or someone else will need to do The Big Clean. That is not what this chapter will teach you, but perhaps why God invented cleaning ladies, cleaning services, and the D.A.—Hmmm, maybe that's what's meant by "cleanliness is next to godliness"?

The Stuff You're Gonna Need

I'm not going to vacuum 'til Sears makes one you can ride on.

—ROSEANNE BARR

Let's be honest . . . our species is not about to get on our hands and knees to clean floors nor roll up our sleeves and blissfully submerge our hands where men's, women's, and children's poop has gone before. So what follows are two lists specifically created for The Cosmetic Clean. The first list contains *Stuff You May Already Have*. The second list itemizes *Stuff You Might Have to Buy*. You'll notice that a key word on the second list is "disposables." That means you can use them and throw them away or plug them in for a fresh clean scent, which makes cleaning a lot more mindless and easy to do. And brands like Clorox, Mr. Clean, Pledge, Lysol, Windex, Fantastic, and Febreze have realized their appeal, so you'll be able to find whatever product you need and the scent you like. Plus, lots of the major supermarket and mass chains now sell their own line of disposable products and buying theirs may save you a few dinero.

As for the *Stuff You May Already Have*—get ready to indulge in some fun and unusual uses that your mother never dreamed would make faucets glow, showers shine, and dust disappear.

FYI: *The Cosmetic Clean Shopping List* is available in a downloadable version on my website www.theaccidentalhousewife.com. Shortened lists based on what follows also accompany the sections for cleaning the bathroom and the rest of the house to help you know what to use for what and limit lugging around that which you don't need!

The Cosmetic Clean Shopping List

Stuff You May Already Have
- Toothpaste
- Alka-Seltzer
- Shaving cream
- Socks
- Fuzzy slippers (closed backs)
- Plastic wrap
- Newspaper
- Loofah gloves
- White wine
- Music
- Scented candles

Stuff You Might Have to Buy
- An array of disposables
  - Dust cloths or sheets
  - Disinfectant multipurpose, multisurface cleaning wipes
  - Toilet brush scrubber with throwaway pads (such as Clorox Toilet Wand, Scrubbing Bubbles Fresh Brush or Scotch Brite Toilet Bowl Scrubbers)
  - Mops and carpet cleaners with throwaway cleaning sheets

and/or spray cleaner attached (such as Swiffer Sweeper, Carpet Flick and Wet Jet, or Clorox Ready Mop)

- Baby wipes
- Cordless stick vacuum
- Paper towels
- Loofah gloves
- White wine
- Music
- Disinfectant air fresheners, scent systems, scented plug-ins

Stuff You Must Buy and Why

The guy with the rubber gloves was surprisingly gentle.

—ACE VENTURA, PET DETECTIVE

Classic and Cool Tools

As homage to our ancestral species, the 1950s' housewife, and our species' desire to maintain our hands and refrain from overworking, every accidental housewife needs to own these two classic cleaning tools:

1. RUBBER GLOVES: For decades they've been a housewife's hands' best friend and they can easily be found in your local supermarket's cleaning products aisle. And, as with most things nowadays, fashion has joined function so you can be styling while you're shining. Diamonds, fur, polka dots, pearls, Pucci, or basic black—there's a pair of rubber gloves that's just right for you! Check out some at: www.royalaccessories.com. My personal picks are the pink ones with black-and-white polka dots and pearls.

2. FEATHER DUSTER: Feather dusters are a timeless and time-tested cleaning tool. They're easy to use, they're a perfect cos-

metic cleaning companion, and they make you feel a bit magical. The true experts recommend ostrich feathers over chicken or synthetic since they believe they hold on to the dust better. Other experts question whether the dust is gone or has simply flown off to a new locale. Then, there is the accidental question: Do we even care?

Smart Tools

This has a few meanings. The first is being smart about buying tools that will help you do any of your cleaning tasks easily and with little toll on your body. These smart tools include all the disposable wipes, sprays, brushes, mops, scents, and so on. They also include lightweight stick vacuums that can be easily carried about and stored for The Cosmetic Clean. For those who are interested in buying a larger, all-purpose vacuum or are in need of one for The Big Clean, you should check out *The Accidental Housewife's Buyer's Guide to Vacuums* on page 9.

The other meaning of smart relates to tools that are actually called "smart" or "intelligent." These are robotic helpers that require you to push a button or two to use them. Then you can sit back, watch the tool work for you, or take a snooze. There are many models out there and you'll want to try to determine which best suits your needs and your wallet. Two to consider are the pocketbook-friendly IRobot Roomba series (www.irobot.com) and the more sophisticated and expensive Electrolux Trilobite (www.electrolux.com). And, coming soon to a McMansion near you, is the future-friendly and pricey humanoid variety: NUVO (www.nuvo.jp). Its creators boast that it walks, talks, takes pictures, and will laugh at your jokes whether they're funny or not. But can it do windows is my question. When it can do that *and* make my favorite cup of coffee it will be a *truly* smart tool.

Portable Schlep Vehicle

Our goal is to make cleaning convenient, brainless, and schlep-free. So in addition to the rubber gloves, feather duster, and portable stick vacuum you should buy at least two easy-to-transport "schlep vehicles" that can hold your main cleaning stuff. These should be stored fully stocked near your high-traffic, high-visibility areas. Consider colorful buckets or baskets with comfy handles, a tool belt, a caddie (as in tool, not golf!), a mini wagon, or whatever "schlep vehicle" works best for you. Some convenient places to store them include:

- Under the bathroom sink
- Under the kitchen sink
- In the family or living room closet

The Accidental Housewife's Buyer's Guide

VACUUMS

We've already established that sometime this century you or a D.A. is going to do *The Big Clean*, which means you're going to need a real vacuum. Think of it like buying a car in terms of style, model, color, size of engine, and you're halfway there! So, with that in mind, some practical tips from my local vacuum store guru Ben and a few accidental housewifely considerations, your guide follows.

According to Ben, the first thing you should do is decide what kind of model you like and what you're going to use it for the most. Model choices do not include portable, cordless, handheld, stick, or broom styles. Ben considers these "toys" and not for the serious vacuumer, which is exactly why they're included in *The Cosmetic Clean's Stuff You Might Have to Buy* list on pages 6–7.

Canister vs. Upright

Fortunately you only have to consider two models: canister and upright. In the old days canisters were considered best for bare floors, stairs, and drapes. Uprights were considered best for rugs and wall-to-wall. But as time goes on, the differences between the two have become less obvious. All the major manufacturers like Miele, Seba, Hoover, Electrolux, Eureka, and Bosch have models that do just about everything at a variety of price points.

Another option is to put in your very own central vacuum system with all the bells and whistles you want. Of course this option may suck up your bank account in addition to the dirt on your floors.

Once you determine whether you prefer canister or upright think about the following:

- Surface: Are you going to use it on hardwood, carpet, or other floor type/covering?
- Construction/Durability: Plastic or metal
- Versatility: Does it work on any kind of floor without special attachments? What is the hose length?—length matters! Does it have tools for vacuuming couches, drapes, etc.?
- Power: How much sucking up do you need?
- Bag or bagless (See All in the Bag page 11.)
- Ease to change bags
- Noisiness

- Size: Will it fit in your closet?
- Weight: Is it hard to lug around?
- Sturdiness: Will it withstand your banging into walls?
- Design/Color
- Special features: Do you need a dust sensor? (Are your eyes not good enough?); Shampooing option; does it have soft hair or vinyl brushes? FYI: Ben says horsehair's the way to go.
- Blow-drying capability: Can you use it to dry your hair?
- Warranty: 3-year minimum recommended
- Price

All in the Bag: Bagless vs. Bag Vacuums

Ben is very passionate about vacuums and he is vehement about not buying bagless vacuums. He says they're messy to empty since unless you're standing directly over the garbage some of the dirt always misses the can. Also, bagless vacuums mean that the dirt's flying all around inside, clogging the filters, which can result in mold and a need to change them more often. To an accidental housewife this is a no-no, since it will mean more cleaning, more filter changes, and spending more money.

On the other hand, Ben loves vacuums that require bags and recommends using only HEPA (High Efficiency Particulate Air) filter bags. They're particularly good for folks with allergies since they trap all those dust mites lurking about and let clean air through. Of course like everything else there are different types available, but Ben's pick is hospital-grade filters, since they're soft and trap the most stuff.

Whether you decide to go bagless or with the bag, you'll be spending money on filters or bags. So my accidental advice is to go with the HEPA and take advantage of the mindless health benefits you'll reap. You'll also make Ben *very* happy!

A Few More Things

- TAKE A TEST DRIVE: Go to a major retailer like Sears or Best Buy, since they carry most models, and try a few out to see which is most comfy for you.
- DON'T WASH YOUR FILTERS: Washing vacuum filters is a *no-no*—it can cause them to shrink or fall apart, or reduce their ability to trap the dirt, since the filter's fibers can stretch out.
- MORE FEATURES, MORE PROBLEMS: Just because a vacuum has lots of different features doesn't automatically mean it's a better machine. In fact, more features mean more things can go wrong. On the flip side Ben believes that you should buy a more expensive machine that has select features, since such machines are built to last and generally come with a longer warranty. REMEMBER: Ben makes his living from selling vacuums, so take this advice with that in mind.

THE AREAS YOU GOTTA CLEAN

I found out why cats drink out of the toilet. My mother told me it's because the water is cold in there. And I'm like, how did my mother know that?

—WENDY LIEBMAN

In the beginning of this chapter you learned that the Numero Uno Cleaning Rule is to *Focus First on High-Traffic, High-Visibility Areas.* As a reminder, these are the bathroom (those used most

WHAT'S YOUR CLEANING HI Q?

Time now to see just how much or little you really know about the world of housecleaning. Introducing the Accidental Housewife's HI Q Test (which stands for Housewife Intelligence Quotient). A fun, frivolous, and short test you'll find in every chapter. Fear not, there are no wrong answers or rankings—just some fun and perhaps useful knowledge to be gained. Answers are below . . . no peeking!

TIP: The first question is not a trick question. It is there to build your confidence. The level of difficulty increases as you go along.

Which task is not considered basic cleaning?

1. Emptying the trash

2. Dusting

3. Vacuuming

4. Polishing nails

5. Cleaning toilets

What is an "intelligent" or "smart" tool?

1. Educated

2. Attractive

3. Robotic

4. Chic

5. Gifted

Which health and beauty aid below cleans toilets best?

1. Preparation H

2. Alka-Seltzer

3. Noxema

4. Midol

5. Sanitary pads*

What's a Dirty Martini?

1. A martini served in a dirty glass
2. An X-rated version of a martini
3. A martini made with olive juice found in the olive jar
4. A martini made with dirt

ANSWERS: 4, 3, 2, 3

* If you choose to get on your knees for any cleaning activity (and why you would escapes me), you can place one pad under each knee for comfort. Do not flush or reuse when done.

often), the kitchen, and major living spaces. Now you'll learn how to clean them without much muss or fuss. As for what time of day is best, I find that right after I've had a cup of coffee and am not in a rush to get dressed, take my son to school, or go to a meeting works well for me, but the key is doing it when you're in the mood and not under the gun. As for when you'll need to move from The Cosmetic Clean to The Big Clean—that will depend on several factors, some of which were mentioned earlier, including:

- Number of folks in your household (the more there are the more quickly it will get dirty)
- Comfort level with dirt
- Amount of company you have
- How much you're home
- Ability to afford a D.A.

Before getting to the first area you gotta clean—the bathroom— I'd like to share a personal tale that has its roots in this room, sort of.

AN ACCIDENTAL ASIDE

Got Gas?

One morning, my family and I were awakened not by the soothing sounds of James Taylor on our Bose, but by the piercing sound of our carbon monoxide and explosive gas alarm. Being a sleeper akin to the princess and the pea, I jumped up frantically and jarred my husband out of his usual dead man's sleep to check out the situation. I did seek his word first that his life insurance premiums were up-to-date. He assured me they were, and I sent him off. Within minutes he returned; having found no leaks, he reset the alarm. All was well.

NOT!! Off again it went and so did I to call our local PSE&G folks. Within a half hour they arrived and went through our house with their handy-dandy detectors searching for the toxic gas I was sure would kill us. Fortunately, they found that nothing toxic was floating about, so to speak. It was then that Mr. PSE&G explained the facts of gas to me: First, explosive gas that can kill you smells and is usually defined as methane and propane. Carbon monoxide cannot be smelled. Second, a far more toxic gas to our nasal sensibilities is that which explodes or is released from our bodies: i.e., farts and poop—which is what he believed caused our alarm to go off.

So the next time your carbon monoxide and explosive gas alarm goes off, check the following before calling your local utility company:

- Who's done what in the bathroom
- Who's got gas, and
- The alarm's batteries

THE END!

Now back to the areas ya gotta clean:

1. The Bathroom

Cleaning the bathroom has to be one of the worst jobs in the world. I mean, really, the thought of putting our hands where stuff only our internist gets excited about touching and analyzing is a gross and terrifying thought. But an accidental housewife's gotta do what an accidental housewife's gotta do, and cleaning doo is part of that job.

Bathroom Stuff You Need Handy

REMINDER: Put all items in schlep vehicle of choice.

- Rubber gloves
- Toothpaste
- Toothbrush
- Foam shaving cream
- Newspaper
- Alka-Seltzer or denture cleaning tablets
- Disposables: toilet brush scrubber
- Disinfectant wipes or baby wipes
- Shampoo
- Loofah gloves
- Spray bottles. (Fill as suggested in the shortcuts that follow.)
- Paper towels
- An old, opened bottle of white wine

Sink-to-Shower Shortcuts

It is recommended that anytime you clean and particularly when doing tasks in the bathroom, you wear rubber gloves. Also, please note that in some instances, more than one cleaning shortcut is provided. Any of them will work; it's a matter of your personal preference.

SINKS AND FAUCETS

- Put a dab of your favorite toothpaste on your toothbrush and one on your faucet. Brush your teeth, then rub the faucet with paper towel. Wipe it off with water and smile: You'll see your pearly whites shining back at you.

  or

- Swipe and wipe faucets and sink with baby wipes, disinfectant wipes, or crumpled newspaper (See *The Dirt on Newspaper* on page 29 for more tips).

MIRRORS

Cover your mirror with foam shaving cream and let it sit for a few minutes, then wipe it off. Believe it or not, it will also keep your mirror defogged for up to three weeks! Follow with a soothing face or leg shave for yourself!

TOILETS

They're probably the worst and yuckiest thing to clean in anyone's house, so the faster we can do it and the farther we can be from it the better.

Fizz, Brush , and Flush

- Plop-plop two Alka-Seltzer or denture tablets (flavored not necessary!) into bowl.
- Fizz-fizz for at least 20 minutes.
- Brush-brush with your disposable toilet brush scrubber.
- Flush-flush along with your flushable pad.

Please note: Depending upon the level of your bowl's distress a second dose may be required.

AN ACCIDENTAL ASIDE

Some people swear that Coca-Cola is a terrific toilet bowl cleaner. After several trials (and cans!), I still prefer mine diet and over ice instead of in the bowl. I have found, however, that it is a pretty good rust remover, which leads me to wonder: If it removes rust, what effect is it having on my insides?

TOILET SEAT AND BOWL EXTERIOR

Clean with household disinfectant cleaning wipes. I prefer not taking any chances by using baby wipes since they are often milder so as to not irritate a baby's butt. Of course, in a pinch they're better than nothing!

TUB AND TILE

Rub-a-Dub-Dub

Squirt some shampoo on a loofah glove and rub that tub and tile's scum away. You can follow up with a disinfectant wipe to further squash those scummy rings. When through, rinse thoroughly. Next remove your rubber gloves and apply your favorite exfoliating gel to your hands and feet. Scrub-a-dub that dead skin away.

SHOWER

Shower and Scour

- Put one capful of baby shampoo into a spray bottle.
- Fill the rest with water.
- Spray.
- Wipe dry with a paper towel.

   TIP: Leave spray bottle in the shower for whenever the mood hits to clean!

Waste Not, Wine Not

Next time you're about to throw away that week-old bottle of white wine, use it to clean your shower door. Pour it into a spray bottle, spray the door, and rinse it off with water. To remove the wine smell, very lightly spray disinfectant air freshener on a paper towel or newspaper and wipe dry. REMINDER: Too much spraying will leave streaks.

You can use white wine vinegar if you've consumed all your old wine.

SHOWER CURTAIN

Most every shower curtain is machine washable. If yours isn't, toss or give it away and buy one that is!

2. The Rest of the House

The Faucet-to-Floor Face-lift: A 20–40 Minute Cosmetic Cleanup

You make the beds, you wash the dishes, and six months later you have to start all over again.

—JOAN RIVERS

It took a bit of trial and error, a few broken nails and misapplied facial treatments, but The Cosmetic Clean routine that follows *really* works. It may take some practice, but along the way you'll have fun, enjoy some pampering, and clean your home easily and painlessly in 20–40 minutes. Time and results will vary per individual depending upon how much you're enjoying the music, the length of time required for your beauty applications, or how long you've let your high-traffic, high-visibility areas collect dirt.

Please remember, this is a "cosmetic" cleanup and will not replace an eventual need to do a more thorough housecleaning sometime in the next six months. It will, however, pass the mother/mother-in-law white-glove test and keep dirt and dust below eye level until the next time you decide to do it or hire a D.A. (See *D.A.s Are da Best* on page 33).

Rest-of-the-House Stuff You'll Need Handy

REMINDER: Put all items in schlep vehicle of choice.

- Rubber gloves
- Feather duster
- Portable or smart vacuum
- Disposables:
  - Dust wipes
  - Disinfectant cleaning wipes
  - Baby wipes
- Plastic wrap
- Socks or fuzzy slippers (closed backs)
- Hand and body lotion
- Music
- Scented something (candles, air freshener, disinfectant spray)
- OPTIONAL: Hair conditioner, facial mask, hair-removal or hair-renewal treatments.

AN ACCIDENTAL ASIDE

Experience has taught me that drinking, dancing, and dusting don't mix, and can prove hazardous to one's health and the face-lift's outcome. Therefore it is recommended that you refrain from any alcoholic beverages or mind-altering substances prior to or during the cleanup.

PRE-CLEAN UP PAMPERING PREP

(Not included as part of cleanup time given)

1. Load your favorite tunes. If possible wear headphones or borrow them. This will ensure solitude and tune everything and everyone else out.
2. Light candles or turn on scented air freshener/purifier.
3. Put lotion on your feet.
4. Wrap feet in plastic.
5. Place socks or fuzzy slippers on feet.
6. Put lotion on your hands.
7. Place hands in rubber gloves.
8. Start music.

Your hand and foot moisturizing treatments are now under way. ENJOY!

OPTIONAL SKIN- AND HAIR-CARE GROOMING TREATMENTS

These are just a few more grooming and beauty treatments for those who wish to multitask even when it comes to their appearance. REMINDER: Treatments may require a bit of practice to apply before being perfected.

- FACIAL MASK: Apply mask per instructions. Confirm that mask should be on a minimum of 20 minutes to preclude any unknown or long-term beauty mishaps.
- HAIR CONDITIONING: Massage or comb conditioner through hair per instructions and wrap in warm, wet towel. Secure with a large hair clip or presentation clip if that helps. Don't cover your ears. You don't want your hair to fall down and impair your vision nor your ability to hear the tunes and dance through this cleanup.
- HAIR REMOVAL: Apply per product instructions. Confirm removal time coincides with face-lift time line to avoid any bodily harm.

> • HAIR GROWTH ENHANCERS: Apply per product instructions. Usually products like Rogaine take 15–20 minutes to absorb—a truly perfect and mindless cosmetic cleanup activity since you don't have to worry about the timing!

LET THE LIFT BEGIN!

It's up to you in which order you choose to do your cleanup, but I always like to ease my way into it and finish with gusto. You don't want to get that heart pumping too hard before it's had a chance to adjust to the trauma of cleaning. To help you get into your groove, I've suggested a room-by-room timing and tempo guide and shared some of my favorite tunes to clean by.

Waltzin' Through the Bedroom

Suggested Cleaning Time: 5 to 10 minutes

Tempo: Select music with a slow to moderate, but inspirational build. My choice is often a tune sung by Andrea Bocelli or James Taylor, or when I need incentive, I play my fave from The Black-Eyed Peas, *"Let's Get It Started."*

- Beds: Puff pillows. Turn up comforter.
- Furniture: Feather dust. Use of dust wipes optional depending upon energy level and mood.
- Floors: Use cordless stick vacuum or smart tool (refer back to *Smart Tools* on page 8 if you need your memory refreshed about what these are). Throw any laundry into hamper, closet, or under bed.
- Children's/Guest bedrooms (if applicable): Repeat steps above or close doors and save for another day.
- *Spray liberally with favorite air freshener when finito.*

Boogyin' in the Bathroom

Suggested Cleaning Time: 5 to 10 minutes

Tempo: Select music with an increasing upbeat tempo that takes your mind far, far away from the yucky task at hand. I often listen to Sheryl Crow's "All I Want to Do Is Have Some Fun," Alicia Keys's "Karma," or Mariah Carey's "Shake It Off."

- Sinks, Counters, Mirrors, and Tubs: Use all-purpose disposable disinfectant cleaning wipes
- Toilet Bowl: Drop two Alka-Seltzer tablets into the bowl. Let dissolve and fizz. If you want to boogie longer or come back later, let them sit in bowl for 20 minutes. Wipe inside with disposable, flushable toilet bowl brush and pad. Wipe outside with disinfectant cleaning wipes.
- Floors: Boogie back and forth with your cordless stick vac to remove any hair and loose dirt.
- *Spray with favorite disinfectant air freshener when done.*

Shakin' in the Kitchen

Suggested Cleaning Time: 5 to 10 minutes

Tempo: Select music that gets your arms moving and body groovin'. I like Prince's "Cinnamon Girl" or Brian Wilson's "Good Vibrations." Hip-hop and rap are a good shakin' tempo, too.

- Countertops, Appliances, and Sinks: Shine 'em up with all-purpose disposable disinfectant wipes.
- Floors: Use cordless stick vacuum to pick up loose dirt and crumbs.
- *Spray with favorite disinfectant air freshener when done.*

Rockin' 'Round the Living Room and Family Room

Suggested Cleaning Time: 5 to 10 minutes

Tempo: Select music that moves you through these rooms with gusto and builds to the grand face-lift finale. I like classic disco tunes like Donna Summer's "Last Dance," Gloria Gaynor's "I Will Survive," or Rihanna's 2005 hit "Pon de Replay."

- Furniture and Lamps:
  - Feather dust.
  - Shine furniture with disposable dust wipes.
- Carpet and Floors:
  - Use cordless stick vacuum to pick up loose surface dirt and smooth carpet if "fluffy" type.
- In addition, for floors only:
  - Lightly dampen disposable dust wipes so you don't slip and hurt yourself on floors.
  - Place wipes under socks or slippers.
  - Dance with those dust bunnies! Slide 'n glide all over the floor. Break dancing permitted.
- *Spray with your favorite disinfectant air freshener when complete.*

One- to Five-Minute Touch-ups

One to Two Minutes:

On the days you feel like spending only a minute or so cleaning, here are a few one- to two-minute tasks. Aptly enough, I like to do these tasks to Chopin's *Minute Waltz,* which actually takes two minutes to play but assures me that I don't spend more time on them than I can handle! FYI, Chopin used the word "minute" to describe that the waltz was small. It is taken from the French word *minute,* which means tiny. Regardless of how you interpret it, these tasks are still short and tiny, too:

- Empty trash.
- Puff pillows.
- Chuck old magazines.
- Stack mail.

Three to Five Minutes:

It's 5 p.m. on a Saturday (do I feel a song coming on?) and you've just received a call from your mom, friend, or significant other telling you they're stopping by. No problem! Empty trash and puff pillows as suggested in One to Two Minutes* tasks and complement by:

- Lighting scented candles or spraying/turning on air freshener.
- Preparing and serving the perfect cosmetic cleaning cocktail. Drinking at least one is guaranteed to make any home look good, and you're following in the spirit of our ancestral 1950s' housewife, who loved martinis!

THE COSMETIC CLEAN DIRTY MARTINI

1½ oz. of ABSOLUT Vodka

1 Splash of Olive Juice

½ oz. of Dry Vermouth

3 Olives (Stuffed optional—though I love the gigando ones filled with blue cheese!)

Stir over ice. Strain into a chilled martini glass. Garnish with olives.

---

*If it's been at least a week since doing the *Faucet-to-Floor Face-lift* you probably should clean the guest bathroom. Don't panic—just clean the sink and the toilet bowl per *Sink-to-Shower Shortcuts* on page 16.

BROKEN GLASS PICKUP TIP

If you or any of your guests get sloppy and drop a glass on a hard floor, use a slice of bread to pick up the slivers. Press it down gently over the pieces, and violà! they'll stick to the bread. Once you've cleaned up the glass, you may want to cut off serving any more of these martinis to he, she, or ye.

Other Stuff You May Like to Know

Not only is there no God, but try finding a plumber on Sunday.

—WOODY ALLEN

The Virtues of Vinegar and Vodka

White vinegar is one of those tried-and-true all-purpose cleaners that no accidental household should be without. In addition to some of the uses mentioned for cleaning (and to being a tasty ingredient in salad dressing, though I prefer red wine vinegar), it's terrific for keeping cutting boards bacteria-free; cleaning your microwave, mirrors, and windows; shining countertops; ridding tiles and tubs of scum and soap; and much, much more. The same holds true for vodka. So what follows are some less apparent but equally effective uses for these versatile "ingredients." They are gathered from fellow accidental housewives, home care experts, and little ole me:

Vinegar's Virtues (Repeat as needed.)
- FRUIT STAIN REMOVER: Get that strawberry juice off your hands by pouring some in your palm and rubbing all over. Wipe with paper towel.
- BEE STING SOOTHER: Saturate a cotton ball and dab or pour directly on sting.

BURN THIS
Housewifely Calorie Counter

The good news about all our housewifely activities is that we burn calories without trying. Here's what's burning when you do The Faucet-to-Floor Face-lift:

FEMALE: 125 lbs.

Moderately and continuously for 20 and 40 minutes

- Dusting: 47; 94
- Vacuuming: 57; 113
- Assorted bathroom cleaning: 72; 144
- Dancing: 85; 170

MALE: 165 lbs.

Moderately and continuously for 20 and 40 minutes

- Dusting: 62; 125
- Vacuuming: 75; 150
- Assorted bathroom cleaning: 95; 190
- Dancing: 112; 225

SOURCE: WWW.CALORIESPERHOUR.COM

- SUNBURN RX: Saturate a soft cloth or pour directly on burn and gently massage.
- HAIR HIGHLIGHTER: For brunettes only: After shampooing, dilute one cup of vinegar with half a cup of warm water in a plastic bowl and rinse. I can't vouch for this one, but my friend Kim swears by it—but, come to think of it, she's a blonde. *Proceed with caution!*
- FLAKE FIGHTER: After shampooing, mix equal parts vinegar and water and rinse to relieve dandruff. Some say it even helps to prevent baldness! If you find it does please let me know as soon as possible since my husband is eager to try some.
- HICCUP TERMINATOR: Take one tablespoon and swallow. Yuck! This tip came to me from my mother-in-law's friend Ruth, who

is eighty-four and swears by it. She also believes in the healing power of chicken soup as so many of us do. *Remember, Ruth is not a doctor, and though it works for her it may not be the best way to cure* your *hiccups, so use your judgment.*

- ONION ODOR EATER: Pour some in palm of hands and rub.
- SHINER: Dampen a cloth with some and shine your patent leather shoes or bags. I guess this will be good to know when patent's back in style!

Vodka's Virtues (Use judgment and repeat as necessary.)

- FACIAL FIXER: Dampen a cotton ball or pad and dab on face to cleanse and tighten pores.
- SORE THROAT RX: Take a shot and gargle with it—also works if you have a toothache. My accidental question is: Are we numbing the pain or our mind? Then, again, does the answer matter?
- CLEAN EYEGLASSES: Keep a little in a spray bottle and spray or just put a drop or two on each lens and wipe with paper towel or newspaper.
- BAND-AID REMOVER: My first thought is: Buy Band-Aids that come off painlessly, but if you choose not to, just put a few drops near the ends and voilà! no loss of hair or skin.
- JEWELRY SPARKLER: Fill a small bowl and soak your gold and diamond jewelry. Scrub with soft toothbrush and see how they glow! And now a word from my jeweler, Bobby of Hartgers! I checked out this technique with him and his first words of advice were not to waste good vodka on cleaning your jewelry. But, if you do, he advises that you use it on only nonporous stones such as diamonds, and precious metals such as platinum and gold and, *never* to clean porous stones like turquoise and pearls.

- FLOWER FRESHENER: Give a "shot" to fresh flowers to kill any bacteria and to keep the water nice and clean.
- HANGOVER HELPER: Freeze half a cup of vodka and half a cup of water in a Ziploc freezer bag to use as a soft ice pack for sprains, aches, black eyes, and hangovers!!!

Bottoms up!

The Dirt on Newspaper

Not only are newspapers among our favorite reading companions when visiting ye throne, they're also a convenient, multipurpose household helper. I know you're often left with newsprint all over your hands, but if you wear rubber gloves or just wash your hands with soap when you're through you'll be happy with the results. Here are a few of newspaper's undercover benefits and uses:

- SHINE FAUCETS/POLISH CHROME: Newspaper ink is a terrific polishing agent. Also, newspaper is lint free, unlike paper towels. Crumple and shine.
- CLEAN MIRRORS AND WINDOWS: Crumple and wipe.
- COLLECT DUST: Crumpling *not* required. Wet edge of sheet lightly, press, and sweep dirt onto it.
- ABSORB ODORS: Place a few sheets in the bottom of garbage can or other odor problem area.
- DRY SNEAKERS: Crumple and leave in each sneak overnight.
- SWAT FLIES: Roll up any section and start swatting!

Friendly Reminder: Try to recycle after reading and using.

AN ACCIDENTAL ASIDE

Learning about the newspaper's many talents gave me pause to ponder: Could it be that the newspaper's odor-absorbing talent is the real reason so many people read it in the bathroom? *Hmmmm.*

Washin' the 'Wave

It's important to take care of what may be the single most important cooking tool in our accidental lives—the microwave. Here's a simple way to rid it of dirt and gook, which will also leave it smelling good:

1. Cut a lemon in half
2. Fill a microwavable dish or cup with a cup (that's 8 oz.!) of water.
3. Squeeze the lemon into the water.
4. Add the lemon halves.
5. Microwave for at least 5 minutes.
6. CAUTION: The dish or cup will be very hot, so use a potholder.
7. Wipe inside yuck off with a paper towel.

Get Sharp

I'm talking as in keeping your blades sharp in your sink's garbage disposal for all the crap you send its way. Here are two easy ways to maintain its edge:

- Put eggshells (not the whole egg) into your disposal and turn it on.
- Make vinegar ice cubes and send them down the drain to be

sliced and diced. They'll also act as a deodorizer. Run cold water through when done.

Please note: This suggestion came from my friend Marcia who has a mega-kitchen and a top-of-the-line sink. And though I have tried it in my disposal and all went well, some disposals may not be suitable for this kind of "sharpening." Therefore, I'd suggest you test your disposal's ability to slice and dice by using a small piece or a chip of ice first to insure that it can handle this and won't destroy your disposal.

Keep Your Sponges Spongeworthy

You can't see 'em, but bacteria love to live and grow in your handy-dandy sponges. You must clean them every week or two unless you like these little critters living among and on you. Here are four simple ways to help get rid of them:

- Put sponges on the top level of your dishwasher.
- Throw them into the washing machine and clean with hot water.
- Sanitize in the microwave for one minute. (Be careful—they'll be hot and still damp!)
- Just chuck and replace with new ones.

Talkin' Trash

Indoor garbage or trash cans are one of the most used items in our homes. They're also one of the most abused. Here are some ideas to help keep them smelling fresh and a few tips for the lazy:

For odors:
- Place an antistatic fabric sheet in can.
- Keep newspaper on bottom.

For the lazy:

- Keep extra bags underneath the bag being used.
- Buy an electronic trash can. There are several affordable models available that open and close with just a wave of your hand. NOTE: You will still need to change the bags and the odors will need tending.

Odor Snuffers

Every household has its share of good and bad smells. This section is for treating those you want to snuff out easily and quickly:

- VANILLA: It's good for the fridge: Just pour a little vanilla extract (you can find it bottled in the baking section of your supermarket) on a cotton ball and put it in a small dish or cup where it won't be disturbed. It's also good for the rest of the house: Put a few balls in small decorative bowls and scatter throughout your home.
- BAKING SODA: You may already know about its benefit for the fridge but it's worth repeating. Just put a freshly opened box in the back of yours and let it go to work. You should put a fresh box in every month. It's also good as a cutting board deodorizer: Make a paste by mixing it with a little water and scrubbing. Yes, it will require your rubber gloves, or you can use an old toothbrush so your hands don't have to touch it. If you have a cat, sprinkle some in its litter box to keep it smelling fresher longer.
- SCENTED SPRAYS AND CANDLES: These are good for all-around-the-house air freshening. There are lots to choose from and they come in all shapes and sizes from sprays to plug-ins to systems like Febreze Scent Stories, which offer an array of scented discs to please your nasal proclivities. And of course you can go for the good old-fashioned scented candle variety.

- POTPOURRI: A tried-and-true way to deodorize. There are even potpourris for vacuums. Try Fragrance Scent from Progressive Sales of Texas—it's very reliable and will help control pet dander or any other yucky smells trapped inside your vacuum bag.
- WINDOWS AND FANS: Open as many as you can without freezing out or overheating your household! Place a fan in the window to get rid of the odor even faster. If it's summertime, be sure you have screens so you don't trade in a fresh home for nasty bugs!

And last but not least ...

D.A.s Are da Best

Throughout this chapter, I have mentioned the D.A.—short for Domestic Assistant—without giving you much info about them other than recommending that *every one of us* should indulge in one when we can afford to for The Big Clean.

Having a D.A. will enable you to maximize the life of your *Sink-to-Shower Shortcuts* and *Faucet-to-Floor Face-lift* as well as your sanity and French manicure. And, unlike plumbers, some D.A.s even work on Sunday! So here's the scoop on what you should think about when hiring a D.A., followed by the garden varieties available to fill your bill:

HASSLE-FREE HIRING HINTS
- Use family, friends, and neighbors to refer folks or services.
- Go online to locate agencies that service your area. Type in "local cleaning services in (your state)."
- Check the Yellow Pages.
- Be sure cleaning services are bonded, insured, and an official member of the Better Business Bureau in your state.

- If you have the time or inclination, get three estimates and haggle!
- Ask if they do laundry—it may come with a small charge but it'll be worth not having to do it!
- VERY IMPORTANT: Be sure they speak the same language as you—even if it's English!

GARDEN-GROWN VARIETIES

No matter which of the following is the right type D.A. for you and your needs, don't forget to get references. Having these may still not mean that you've found your very own Mrs. Doubtfire, but they will weed out those who don't even come close.

- THE SOLO CLEANER: They're usually referred to you by friends, family, or neighbors. Their only job is cleaning homes, which may also include doing your laundry—so ask! They usually spend three to six hours cleaning depending on the size of your home. Fees vary but you should ask your buds what they're paying so you know what to expect.
- THE CLEANING CORPS: *"Many Hands Make Light Work"* is their motto: Cleaning corps or cleaning services usually have two or more individuals who come to your home. They arrive via van or SUV and spend two to five hours there depending on the size of your home. Some bring their own cleaning products, but what they bring could be limited and there could be a fee, so inquire. Generally you are one of several jobs they are doing in a day. Fees vary according to the amount of work, size of your home, etc. Some will have a menu of prices available on their website while others will ask you to call them for an estimate—which should be free!
- NANNIES: Depending on their job descriptions and what you've

agreed to, these individuals usually live in your home and are tasked with all of your housewifely jobs. *I repeat:* If you can afford one, they are your best answer to fulfilling your pre-accidental hopes and dreams. Fees vary and may include a finder's fee for the agency.

Stop Here!

That wasn't so bad, was it? You danced, you sang, you dusted, and you disturbed just enough dirt to keep your abode from being visited by health inspectors. Hopefully, this chapter has made Task #1 a bit less ungodly and your home a bit easier to maintain between visits from your soon-to-be-hired D.A. Now, stir yourself a Dirty Martini and take a break. Your next lesson on how to overcome housekeeping hysteria can wait.

Task #2
LAUNDRY

HONEY, I SHRUNK THE LAUNDRY!!

L aundry . . . you hate living with it and you can't live without it being done . . . unless you don't mind piles of it surrounding you or you throw your clothes away after every wear. And though that might be a nice fantasy, the reality is that laundry—from washing to drying to ironing—is another necessary task that our species is expected to conquer. And conquer it we can by putting our accidental spin on the drudgery of doing it! Unfortunately, unlike cleaning your house, the word disposable doesn't apply to your laundry, and unless you're a CSI wannabe when it comes to stain removal, laundry is pretty straightforward and therefore boring. But, as you may suspect, I've found a light at the end of our laundry vent: I've discovered that doing laundry "accidentally" tones our body, funds facials, *and* can teach us which varietals go best with each laundry cycle. Of course, I'll also help you "see the light" when it comes to ensuring that your Hanes don't shrink or turn from blue to white, or that your favorite shirt doesn't disintegrate when you try removing coffee, wine, or baby spit. So, tumble on.

THE ACCIDENTAL HOUSEWIFE'S LAUNDRY BASICS

Housework can't kill you, but why take a chance?

—PHYLLIS DILLER

In order to do your laundry as effortlessly and efficiently as possible you are going to need a bunch of basic stuff and a few helpful reminders. The first thing is to remember that more is less when buying basics—more on that shortly. The second important thing is to make the task of doing laundry a seamless activity that blends into your everyday schedule, lifestyle, and desire to do it. The third thing is to realize that except for the occasional stain, store-bought stain removers and your machines will do most of the work for you.

Numero Uno Laundry Rule: *Don't Overload*

This rule doesn't need much explaining. But it's an important rule, since the bigger those piles become, the more stressed and angry you'll be. I know it's time to do a load when either I can't find my favorite undies or my son's out of jeans. Each of us will have our own threshold of pile buildup. Just remember that the longer you let it go, the more of a chore it will become.

Here's how to prevent a mental and physical "overload":

- MAKE IT MINDLESS: Pick a convenient time to do it with few or no pressing distractions. Times to consider: getting ready in the morning, watching TV, exercising at home, or during mealtime. CAUTION: Though it may seem like a good time to take a quick jog or go out for a cup of coffee, you should never put a load of laundry into the washer or dryer and leave your home. Though a rarity, floods and fires can occur and that would be overstepping our "accidental" bounds.

- SORT AND ABORT: Do only one wash at a time of white, light, dark, heavy, or delicate stuff. You can do another load later or to-morrow. Simple sorting techniques follow in the Sort 'Em section on page 54.
- TUMBLE 'N TONE: You probably never realized it, but from the moment you've started to do a load, you've started stretching, lifting, and bending—all forms of exercise. More on this as you laundry on.
- TIME IT: Often I forget that I've put a wash in and it sits for hours, causing a mildew smell and more wrinkles. That means more work for Mama—not a "good thing." Use your kitchen timer or any other that you'll hear to remind you that your laundry is finito.

The Stuff You're Gonna Need

What follows is the whole enchilada. It's a lot of stuff, but once you have it you'll be good to go for a while. It includes necessities like detergent, bleach, softeners, laundry baskets, and plastic-coated safety pins. And I've suggested a few "excessities" for your accidental laundry list to lighten the load and the task.

Following the list, I thought it would be helpful for those looking to buy a new washer and dryer to get the scoop on what to consider buying to fit your lifestyle and needs.

FYI: *The Whole Enchilada Laundry List* is available in a downloadable version on my website www.theaccidentalhousewife.com. Shortened lists also accompany washing, drying, and ironing to help you know and remember what to use for what, limit lugging, or avoid using that which you don't need!

The Whole Enchilada Laundry List:

Necessities:

- Prewash stain removers (See *PMS Removal Guide* on page 61.)
- Fine-washable Woolite fabric wash
- Liquid or powder detergent
- Chlorine bleach—for white wash only
- Color-safe non-chlorine bleach—for color wash
- Fabric softener dryer sheets
- Wrinkle releaser
- Different colored laundry baskets, hampers, or bags; wheels optional
- Non-rusting/plastic safety pins, clips, machine-washable sock or lingerie bag
- Plastic hangers
- Plastic storage containers

Optional:

- Starch: Not a must-have on my list, but if you're truly ambitious and want to do your own linens or significant other's dress shirts, go for it!

Excessities:

- Piggy bank
- Full-length mirror
- Tennis balls
- Music system of any sort

When all else fails or not in the mood either drop off at laundromat or call your local pickup and delivery.

- Dry cleaner: Check care label on items first to be sure your stuff is OK to dry-clean.

The Accidental Housewife's Buyer's Guide

LAUNDRY MACHINES

Many of you may already have a washer or dryer, so you can skip right over this. But for those of you who don't or are thinking about buying new appliances, I checked with product experts at Kenmore and Whirlpool and I added some of my personal thoughts to help you figure out which model is right for your needs and your space.

Here are the key things to think about:

- Front load vs. top load (See "The Scoop," page 44)
- Size: Needs to fit into the space you have.
- Capacity
- Noisiness
- Energy conservation
- Ease of operation
- Easy to read
- Is it workout-friendly
- Color/Design
- Price

Gas or Electric? (For Dryers only)

Dryers don't vary all that much. Main differences are noise, capacity, and how they're fueled, i.e., gas or electric. Gas dryers often cost slightly more, but they make up for it in fuel savings over the long term. As for some folks' need for speed-dry, ask yourself what I did: "Do I really want to get to folding sooner rather than later when I could be relaxing or doing what I enjoy for a longer period of time?" The choice is yours, but you don't need to spend more for lots of drying options.

The Scoop on Front Load vs. Top Load

Front-Load Pros:
- Dries quicker: Spins clothes faster so they come out drier.
- Conservation-friendly: Uses less water.
- Saves money:
  - Energy bills
  - Soap
- Easier on clothing, tumbles freely vs. agitates.
- Quieter
- Stackable
- Larger capacity
- Workout-friendly

Front-Load Cons:
- More costly
- Fewer models
- Soap selection limited (See An Accidental Aside: HE Said, I Said on page 45.)
- Learning required
- Price

NOTE: As with all appliances, manufacturers are constantly making improvements, so top load and front load may eventually share many of the same benefits including their price.

AN ACCIDENTAL ASIDE

HE Said, I Said

As an accidental housewife who wants to do fewer and fewer loads of laundry, I purchased a front-load washer with bigger capacity. This also led me to learn about HE—short for High Efficiency. HE means your washer uses less water and energy and you use less detergent. That's a good thing. The problem is that finding HE detergents can be difficult, since not all the major brands make them. Where I live they're incredibly hard to find, which means I have to go searching for them in several stores—not a "good thing." This inspired me to ask the question: What would happen if I used my good ole liquid non-HE stuff? Well, I did, and after using it several times, I can't find any difference in my wash, *yet*. I've also found that since my front-load washer uses less water than my top loader did I don't have to use as much detergent. I must share with you, however, that my machine's manufacturer and favorite laundry detergent manufacturer have warned me that my day of reckoning is coming. They claim the non-HE stuff is not formulated for a HE washer and therefore isn't getting my clothes as clean. I will let you know if and when my day of reckoning comes. I hope if it does, I can find HE stuff more easily.

Stuff You Wanna Know

Stick Them Together

I've got stacks of orphan socks thanks to the infamous Bermuda Sock Triangle that seems to exist in every laundry room. A simple way to save your pairs from separation anxiety is by attaching them with a safety pin or clip, or putting them into a washable laundry, lingerie, or sock bag. If you're like me and don't have the patience to attach each pair individually, use jumbo plastic-coated safety pins or clips.

SHOW OFF THEIR INDIVIDUALITY!

I never used to look at my orphan socks as potential works of art until I visited my friend Teri's house and saw she had framed her family's singles and hung them on the walls of her laundry area. It's a fun and inexpensive way to decorate your apartment or hall walls—not to mention that they make great conversation pieces. For those of you who are handy, buy ready-made frames and frame them yourselves. Another idea is to hang them from wire or a clothesline using decorative clothespins from Tuff & Tidy, which you can find at Bed Bath & Beyond. Or, if you're like me, have someone else frame or hang them for you!

Size Up the Situation

As in all our housewifely endeavors, our rule of thumb is to make things easy and minimize our time spent doing them. So, supersize the basic stuff you gotta get. Sometimes supersize items are referred to as "economy size," which may mean they're also cheaper, but not always—so it's good to check. Plus, buying the supersize means fewer trips to the supermarket, *and* lifting and pouring these biggies will help build upper body strength!

If you live in a small apartment, have no washer and dryer in it, and/or have to lug all your stuff up and down stairs or elevators every time you do a load, stick with the regular size products. You may not save some money, but you'll save your back and the money you'd spend on trips to the chiropractor.

Follow Your Nose!

How do you know which laundry cleaning product is right for you? Truth is, my fellow housewifely launderers and I have found that liquid or powder, name brand or generic, each product performs pretty much alike. What differs are your machine's requirements, product price, the form they may come in (liquid, powder, tablet or ball), scent, multitasking benefits (stain fighter, color-safe bleach, etc.), and environmental claims. So choose yours by following directions, your nose, your needs, your wallet, or Mother Earth, and all will be fine.

Talk the Talk

An important step to conquering this housewifely task is to learn what I refer to as "laundry speak." It's that unspoken language that not only separates darks and lights but comes in the guise of one- to two-inch tags printed in mouse-size type that are hidden somewhere—corners, collars, edges, seams, and any other hard-to-find location—and are on everything you own! Their real name is "care label," but what's written on them looks like ancient hieroglyphics, and unless decoded properly could cost you dearly. I learned to "care" the hard way after my favorite white lace undies came out yellow and my husband's Jockeys were reduced to toddler size.

To help you avoid such travesties, I've gone to the experts at TIDE and have included their recent laundry care guide. A downloadable version is available on my website at www.theaccidentalhousewife .com. Please note that though most of the symbols are universal, I have found that some symbols on my clothes do not always match those found on the chart, so read carefully, and good luck interpreting!

TALK THE TALK LAUNDRY CARE GUIDE

The Language of Laundry

Machine Wash Instructions	Special Care	Bleaching Instructions	Dryer Instructions		Ironing Instructions	Dry Cleaning
Normal Wash	Hand Wash	Bleach as Needed	Normal Dry	DO NOT Machine Dry	Low Heat	Dry Clean
Permanent Press	DO NOT Wring	Non-Chlorine Bleach as Needed	Permanent Press	Line Dry	Med. Heat	Dry Clean w/Any Solvent
Gentle Cycle		DO NOT Bleach	Gentle Setting	Drip Dry	High Heat	Dry Clean w/Petroleum Solvent
DO NOT Machine Wash			DO NOT Tumble Dry	Dry Flat	DO NOT Steam	Dry Clean w/Solvents Other Than Trichloroethylene
Cold (<85° F)			No Heat	Dry in Shade	DO NOT Iron	DO NOT Dry Clean
Warm (<105° F)			Low Heat			
Hot (<120° F)			Normal/ Med. Heat			
Hot (<140° F)			High Heat			

Source: www.tide.com

Sorting Wines with Your Wash

This is advice that makes laundry a task worth doing. It's expert advice and suggestions from my friend and wine aficionado Sandra Muller, otherwise known as The Wine Chick. Throughout this task and the book, Sandra will share suggestions on which varietals go best with various housekeeping activities that we do. For example, should you sip a glass of Shiraz while sorting through your darks, a crisp Pinot

WHAT'S YOUR LAUNDRY HI Q?

What is the average number of loads a family does per week?*

1. 0–2
2. 3–5
3. 6–8
4. 9–11
5. Too many

What's the best way to clean baseball caps?

1. Washing machine
2. Dry-clean
3. Woolite in sink
4. Dishwasher
5. Buy a new one

Which is a natural alternative to bleach?

1. Baking powder
2. Lemon
3. Soy milk
4. Vanilla
5. Nothing

What task should hairspray not be used for?

1. Stopping pantyhose runs
2. Removing ink stains
3. Killing bugs
4. Freshening air
5. Styling hair

* According to The Tide Clothesline at www.clothesline.com the average household washes 7.4 loads—about 50 lbs. per week.

What does "colorfast" mean?

1. Works quickly
2. Bleeds
3. A new fast-drying marker
4. Type of Etch-A-Sketch game
5. Doesn't fade or run

ANSWERS: 3, 4, 2, 4, 5

Grigio while cleaning stains, or an Italian sparkling wine while munching on Chinese take-out food? Important info that you may indeed want to know!

The Load Down On . . .

DETERGENTS: LIQUID VS. POWDER

As discussed in *Follow Your Nose!* on page 47, it's really a matter of preference since they basically clean equally. I find liquid's easier and less messy to use than powder. Nowadays there are also tablets and balls to choose from, which make figuring out how much you need almost mindless, more convenient, and mess-free.

FABRIC SOFTENERS: LIQUID VS. DRYER SHEET

Their purpose is to decrease static cling, reduce wrinkles and drying time, and make your stuff softer and fluffier. Here's my take on liquid:

- I've found that liquid fabric softeners build up in my washer, which yucks up the dispenser and means I have to clean it.
- I have to remember to add them since this usually should be done during the rinse cycle.
- I've found that they leave a filmy residue on certain clothing and towels.

FAB USES
for Fabric Dryer Sheets

BUGS BE GONE

- Avoid the sting of those nasty mosquitoes by rubbing a sheet all over your body.
  Please note: Before applying anything on your body, always check the ingredients list of the product you are using as you may be sensitive to some of the listed ingredients. And, to be 100 percent safe, **never** use this technique on children or the elderly.
- Golfers even keep one in their back pocket to keep the bees away.
- Lay a sheet near an ant pile or mouse house and see them flee.

FRESHEN UP EVERYTHING

- Place a sheet in the bottom of your garbage, laundry, or diaper container and change weekly.
- Place a sheet in your sneaks or shoes overnight.
- Put one in your shirt and pants and you'll smell good, too!
- Stash one in dresser drawers.
- Keep one under the seat in your car.

QUICKIE CLEAN UPS

- Use for a Cosmetic Clean dusting.
- Wipe off soap scum in showers.
- Remove static electricity from television and computer screen.

MISCELLANEOUS USES

- Rub pantyhose to eliminate static cling.
- Collect pet hair by rubbing area on clothing.
- In winter, keep one in your coat pocket or jeans to avoid "shocks."

These things led me to switch to fabric softener dryer sheets, which suit my accidental ways better since they're:

- Neater: I don't have to worry about spilling anything.
- Mindless: I can just throw one in at the beginning of the cycle so I don't have to remember anything midway through.
- Light: There are no bottles to lug around or store.

You'll decide which works best for you, but my accidental choice is the dryer sheet.

WRINKLE RELEASERS

Name sort of says it all on this one—they're best when used on dry clothes that have minor wrinkles since they basically relax the wrinkle. If you want a pressed look, you or someone else will have to iron. They also have a nice fresh scent. It's a good idea to check the back of the container to see if there are any fabrics you shouldn't use it on. If you're still not sure, test by spraying an inside corner or area that isn't seen easily.

NOTE: Dryer sheets have lots of terrific nonlaundry uses, which you can learn about in *Fab Uses for Fabric Dryer Sheets* on page 51.

CREATING A WORKOUT SPACE

Organizing Your Stuff

Though more is less when it comes to buying the basics, the opposite holds true in the organization of our laundry area. What we want to do is make it a space that enables us to get the work done and "accidentally" work out at the same time.

Stuff You're Gonna Need

- Plastic bins, crates, boxes, or baskets
- Padded ironing board
- Plastic hangers and hooks
- Full-length mirror
- Facial fund container
- Music system of choice

Stuff You Gotta Set Up

- STORAGE AREA: Get plastic crates or baskets for detergents, bleach, etc., to keep near machines. If you're cramped for space, aren't too short, have long arms, and have a handy person available, put up shelves above your laundry machines.
- FLAT WORK SPACE: For sorting and folding. A great space saver and double-duty work space is an ironing board. If you keep the tops of your machines clear you can also use them.
- WALL OR DOOR HANGINGS: Must be visible for you to easily see. TIP: If you are farsighted, keep an extra pair of reading glasses handy.
  - *Guides: Talk the Talk Laundry Care Guide* (you can copy it from this book, page 48, or print it from my Web site at www.theaccidentalhousewife.com). Also, The Machine Usage Guide that came with your washer or dryer (if available).
  - *Hooks:* Need to be strong enough to hold plastic hangers with damp items on them. Remember: Wet weighs more.
  - *Mirror:* Read Tumble 'n Tone, which follows.

- TUMBLE 'N TONE AREA: If you have a door, hang a long mirror that allows you to see yourself bending, stretching, lifting, and folding. Plug in a radio or sound system of choice.
- FACIAL FUND CONTAINER: Keep an old jar, piggy bank, or cup for change, buttons, etc. You'll be surprised at how much money you've "laundered," and how soon you'll be scheduling a facial, hair replacement treatment, or massage. Remember to check pockets—those $5s, $10s and $20s don't always fall to the bottom of the machine like loose change does.

Now let's get down to the ABCs of laundry.

A. WASHIN'

Step One: Sort 'Em

Separating Darks, Lights, and Varietals

Now that you have an awareness about care labels and "laundry speak," it's time to get your laundry sorted, facial fund started, and workout begun.

First things first:

- COLOR-CODE: Make it a habit or rule that from the moment it leaves anyone's body, table, or wherever, it gets tossed into a color-coded laundry receptacle—you want one each for whites, lights, and darks. Other categories and the space you can allocate are up to you, though I'd recommend including one for fine washables. Make sure everyone in your household knows which is which under penalty they will do all the laundry for the next month.

- THROW IN THE TOWEL: You can throw them in with like colors but not fine washables, since they usually require a longer and more aggressive wash and dry cycle. If you're feeling ambitious, wash separately to avoid lint buildup on other stuff.
- SEPARATE FINE WASHABLES: These are items like bras, fancy undies, hosiery, lingerie, cashmere, wool, linen, spandex, and knits. They usually require gentler detergents and gentler washing. In your mother's day this used to mean hand washing or professionally laundering them, but today's machines generally have a gentle or delicate cycle that won't beat up your fine washables or melt your bra straps.

A Few More "Fine" Points for Fine Washables

WHICH WASH WORKS BEST?

- Woolite Hand and Machine Fabric Wash: It's the gold standard and even comes in a HE version—if you can find it!
- Crabtree & Evelyn Rosewater Laundry Wash: I love this product. I use it on everything since it's gentle and smells so good!

HOW BEST TO WASH AND DRY 'EM?

- BAG 'EM! Put bras, hosiery, and lingerie in a wash bag. The bags don't cost very much and they'll save you from having to buy new bras, etc. as often. They can be found online at www.BedBathand Beyond.com or www.drugstore.com. I even discovered a cube to keep bras in shape called The Bag Company Washing Bra Bag. Check it out at www.lnt.com (that's Linen 'n Things website).
- HANG 'EM! If you feel like it, let your bras, hosiery, and undies air-dry on a plastic hanger or hang them on a bathroom rod to avoid shrinkage, loss of elasticity, or melting of any plastic stuff.

Second things next:

Tumble 'n Tone: Sort Cycle (Skip if Not in the Mood or Interested.)

Trust me, this won't wear you out, but it will help you get through this cycle. I suggest you visit my website at www.theaccidentalhousewife .com and watch my very own *Tumble 'n Tone* video first to avoid any unnecessary stress, strain, or injury. Remember, this is *my* workout and not that of a professional trainer, so use it as a guide and do what feels right for you. Should you choose not to view the video first: Bend from your knees and not your waist. And don't lift more than you can handle—no one's watching!

Begin with one set of five repetitions each. Increase or decrease over time according to number of loads and interest. Musical accompaniment recommended.

Warm-Up:
- Breathe in and out.
- Stretch arms straight overhead, then to the right, then to the left.
- Lean over and touch toes with hands. Return to standing.
- Place hands on hips, bend and squat so knees point outward.
- Stretch neck. Right. Center. Left. Back. Hold each position for 3–5 seconds.
- Rehydrate: drink some water.

Tumble 'n Tone-Up:
- Bend.
- Lift laundry. (For more advanced workoutees: bend and lift at same time.)
- Jog or walk briskly to laundry area. (Depending upon distance, continue moving for 3–5 minutes.)
- Rehydrate: drink some water.

Cool Down:

- Separate stained items: Pretreat per PMS Guide on page 61.
- Zip it: Zip zippers and button buttons to limit damage.
- Rehydrate: Drink some water.

Step Two: Spot 'Em!

The Good, The Borderline, and The Hopeless

Now they show you how detergents take out bloodstains, a pretty violent image there. I think if you've got a T-shirt with a bloodstain all over it, maybe laundry isn't your biggest problem. Maybe you should get rid of the body before you do the wash.

—JERRY SEINFELD

This section may seem more like a lesson in forensics or hurricanes than laundry, but it will help you deal with three categories of stains, learn how to judge each, and how to select which wines work best with several of them.

PLEASE NOTE: The *Tumble 'n Tone-Up* workout has been temporarily replaced with an occasional spotting and tasting activity, which leads me to another personal tale:

AN ACCIDENTAL ASIDE

Grape Expectations from the Mouth of a Babe

I hate to admit it, but I learned this tip from my son's eleven-year-old pal, Keith. He had asked me to explain what my book was about and when I was done (three days later!!!), he replied, "Oh, you mean like how white wine removes red wine stains?" Shocked by both my good fortune in hearing this perfectly wonderful accidental tip and that it was coming from a child, I quickly asked how he knew that. He replied, "My mom told me." Relieved, I finished my Snapple and eagerly awaited my chance to try it out.

Later that afternoon, I decided to indulge in a red wine staining and tasting activity. I called Sandra aka The Wine Chick, who recommended that I pour a food-friendly Chianti onto my tablecloth for the test and of course a little into a glass for me. I then let it set for a few minutes. Sandra had selected an inexpensive Santa Christina Chianti ($10–$13), since she felt it would do the trick and, more important, because she knew I was having pasta for din-din.

Next, I uncorked a day-old bottle of white and poured that on the stain. It took more than a dab to do it, a few shakes of salt, and a spin in the laundry, but good news, it works.

As for which white wine to use if you don't have any bottles open, Sandra suggests using a low-sugar light white such as a Pinot Grigio or a Sauvignon Blanc. Here are two inexpensive picks ($8–$12) to have handy:

- Valverde Pinot Grigio
- Buena Vista Sauvignon Blanc

FYI: If you spill white wine just apply some club soda and wash as usual, or so Keith tells me!

We continue . . .

Stain Removal Stuff You Gotta Get

The best news about all this (other than going to your dry cleaner or hiring a D.A.) is that there are lots of store-bought stain removers available that will take care of most stains. The other good news is that for those that require a little bit more TLC, you can use stuff that you probably already have in your bathroom, kitchen, and bar.

Nonaccidental types suggest attacking stains when they happen so they don't set. They also recommend that you don't put items with stains in the dryer untreated since it will cause the stain to become a permanent embellishment. I've learned the hard way that leaving a stain untreated and putting the item in the dryer is a no-no, so please heed this advice.

Store-Bought Stain Removal Must-Haves
- Shout, Spray 'n Wash (spray or stick), Tide to Go (removes stains instantly—love that!), Zout (liquid or spray), or other favorite stain removal product
- Wine Away*
- Clorox Bleach Pen (for whites only)
- Powdered dishwashing detergent

Hopefully these will be the only stain removal products you will ever need, but if more gusto is required, here are some of my accidental housewifely favorites, listed alphabetically, to help you get those stubborn suckers out. Please refer to the *PMS Removal Guide* on page 61 to see how to use these.

Homegrown Stain Removal Must-Haves
- Baby shampoo
- Club soda
- Emery board
- Hairspray
- Ice cubes
- Liquid hand sanitizers

---

*Wine Away. It's name's a bit of a misnomer. It is great for red wine stains, but also terrific for blood, grape and cranberry juice, and tomato-based stains: chili, ketchup, salsa, tomato sauce, etc.

- Nail polish remover
- Pantyhose
- Potato
- Toothbrush
- Toothpaste
- Salt
- Shaving cream
- Vodka
- White wine
- White wine vinegar

Alternatively:
- Dry cleaner on Speed Dial!

Friendly Reminder

Before attempting any stain removal shortcut, always remember to check care labels for colorfastness and other important instructions. And *never* rub—dabs or blots will usually do!

Step Three: Load 'Em

You've sorted. You've spotted. Now it's time to fill 'er up and get washing. As you begin loading, the key is to remember: DON'T OVER-LOAD. If you do, it can reduce the cleanliness of your laundry, damage your washer, *and* cause you to have to do more work . . . which is not what this book is about.

Here are few more Dos and Don'ts before you get washin':

DOS
- Wash like colors with one another and whites with whites.
- Wash fine washables separately.
- Check pockets for moola.

THE PMS REMOVAL GUIDE

What follows is your PMS Removal Guide. PMS in this case is painless and doesn't affect anyone's hormonal balance. It stands for Pretty Manageable Stains, since it includes the most common and easily handled ones that we accidental housewives may confront.

CATEGORY 1: THE GOOD

I have found that a majority of the everyday stains we'll deal with on items that are *not* fine washables (i.e., bras, hosiery, cashmere, etc.) can be easily pretreated or immediately ousted with the store-bought stain removers. Please note that the makers of several of these products caution us that they don't work well on rust, dried paint, permanent ink, fluorescent clothing, or silk . . . seems silk is the only one that we may care about.

My accidental housewifely advice is that before you start breaking any kind of sweat or experience any mental anguish try one of the store-bought products listed or others that you may know and like. If that doesn't work, proceed to Category 2, which follows.

CATEGORY 2: THE BORDERLINE

If you're reading this I guess the store-bought products didn't get it done. Sorry! But fear not, the shortcuts that follow are for the Top 20 stains you might encounter and they're fairly painless. I still like to apply the store-bought stain removal products after I've given the stains my TLC and before I throw the items in for their final wash. You'll decide if that's necessary. Also, unless noted otherwise, when it says "Rinse," do so in cool water.

For easy reference, the list is in alphabetical order.

- **BABY SPIT:** Soak in cold water or wet and blot with dishwashing detergent.

- BEER: Mix one cup vinegar with two cups water. Blot. Rinse.
- BLOOD: Hit it immediately with cold water until most of it washes out. If it's yours, and you're not hemorrhaging, spit on it and dab or dampen stain and sprinkle with salt. Leave for a bit. Rinse. REMEMBER: The sooner you treat a stain, the greater your chances are of removing it.
- CHOCOLATE: Spoon off excess, dab with baby wipes or liquid hand sanitizer and rinse thoroughly in cold water.
- COFFEE: Gently work in shampoo or hand sanitizer. Rinse with cold water.
- DEODORANT: Rub with pantyhose, foam from dry cleaner hangers, or baby wipes.
- GRASS: Dab with a cloth "drunk" with vodka or apply toothpaste; rub and rinse thoroughly.
- GUM: Freeze area with ice cube. Scrape off excess with dull knife.
- GREASE: Dab with hand sanitizer and rinse. On suede, gently buff with emery board.
- INK STAINS: Saturate with aerosol hairspray and blot with a sponge or paper towel. Rinse thoroughly.
- LIPSTICK: Blot with petroleum jelly or saturate with hairspray. Rinse.
- MAKEUP: Gently rub in a small amount of foam shaving cream or saturate with hairspray, blot and rinse until stain disappears.
- MUD: Use a spud! Cut it in half and gently rub. Soak in cool water.
- NAIL POLISH: Use nail polish remover, but test fabric first to be sure it won't take color out. Put on back of stain and have several paper towels under front to catch polish. It may take a while and several tries. Rinse and put in laundry. Alternate: Douse with hairspray, blot with paper towel, repeat as necessary. FYI: Depending on the depth of color, it may not work.
- RED WINE: Dab with white wine and sprinkle with salt.
- TOMATO-BASED STAINS: Use hand sanitizer, water, or dash of powdered dish detergent, and scrub gently with toothbrush. Rinse.

- **SOY SAUCE:** Flush with club soda or hand sanitizer.
- **TEA:** Wipe gently with hand sanitizer.
- **WHITE WINE:** Dab with club soda or white vinegar. Rinse in cool water.
- **WAX:** Let dry, place paper towel or wax paper on wax and press with iron or freeze with ice cube and chip off excess. Works for crayon stains, too.

CATEGORY 3: THE HOPELESS

If you're reading this section—GIVE UP! Either send it off to your dry cleaner and hope for the best, turn it into a rag, or if you just can't part with it, try one of the following cover-ups:

For clothing:
- Put on a pin, brooch, flower, scarf, iron-on patch, sweater, or jacket.
- Cut the sleeves—turn a long-sleeved item into a short-sleeved item.

For table linens:
- Conceal with a centerpiece or candles .
- If handy or artsy, embroider or patch.
- Cut tablecloth into napkins.

- Pretreat any PMS Category 1 or Category 2 stains.
- Put full loads in per machine capacity.
- Add the proper amount of laundry product according to machine type and fabric care instructions.
- Check care label to choose right cycle and water temp. If you're too lazy and want to chance it, rule of thumb is:
  - Whites: Hot or warm
  - Lights and Darks: Warm or cold
  - Permanent Press: Cold
  - Delicates: Cold
  - Wool: Cold

DON'TS

- Don't put whites in with darks.
- Don't forget to look at Talk the Talk Laundry Care Guide on page 48.
- Don't throw away week-old wine: Use it to remove stains or for stews or risotto.

And, most important don't overload:

- Top-load washers: Stuff no higher than the agitators.
- Front-load washers: Capacity varies. Read individual instructions.

Other Stuff You Might Like to Know

A WINNING WAY TO WASH BASEBALL CAPS

Most guys wear their favorite baseball cap until it falls off their head or they get lice. But, for those who prefer a nice, clean, fresh-smelling one, help is near your kitchen sink! Forget the washing machine, hand-washing, or the dry cleaner, just load the top shelf of your dishwasher with that scummy topping and hit the switch! No shrinking, no fading, no lint. Use a lemony-scented detergent and you'll cover all the bases! FYI: Since all dishwashers are not created equal, you may need to finish drying your hat in the dryer. If so, and if you have one, place it on the nontumble tray to help maintain its shape. For your truly anal cap wearer who worries about shape-shifting, you can find plastic "cap caddies" like the Sportcap Buddy to place hats on whilst washing. Just go online and type in "Sportcap Buddy" to find out where you can buy one.

KEEPING SNEAKS WHITE 'N CLEAN

Unlike baseball caps, I prefer it when my white sneakers get that lived-in, dirty look, as does my son. But for those of you who have kids who make mud, dirt, and grime their sneaks' best friend, or if you're a neatnik who can't wear your canvas or leather sneaks unless they're perfectly clean, here are a few simple ways to restore their gleam:

1. POLISH: Use damp rag to get excess dirt off. Apply white shoe polish on white areas.

2. SCRUB: Remove excess dirt with damp rag. Use toothbrush and scrub with a nonabrasive cleaner like Ajax liquid laundry detergent or Murphy Oil Soap. A Clorox Bleach Pen is also a good whitening tool for stains, and believe it or not, try scrubbing your sneaks with shaving cream—it really works!

3. MACHINE WASH: Only if the label says you can and if you can stand the noise from their tumbling about. Stuff with newspaper to dry overnight, or if you have a dryer with a rack, place them on there so the tumbling noise doesn't drive you nuts. NOTE: Experts are *not* big fans of machine washing sneaks since it can loosen glue, those with Velcro can collect stuff making it less effective, and doing so beats up your machine.

4. DISHWASH: Pretty much the same as doing them in your washing machine except that you should put them on the top rack as you run them through the standard wash cycle. Again, read if they are "machine-washable," so you don't ruin anything. Stuff with crumpled newspaper to dry and maintain shape.

5. SHOP: Buy a new pair and save yourself the work.

If your sneaks have Velcro closures, you're done with this section. If they have laces, you should wash them along with your sneaks or buy new ones.

A NEW SPIN FOR AN OLD STANDBY

No one ever said the washing machine just had to be used to do laundry. Here's a new spin that will surely make it a more appreciated appliance: Fill it with ice and use it as an additional ice chest and wine bar. When the party's over let the water melt, and put on the rinse cycle to drain.

PLEASE NOTE: This usage is **NOT** appropriate for front-load washers.

Here are a few of The Wine Chick's picks to sort through when you decide to use your old standby for a party. The wines she's picked will go with just about anything you serve or can be enjoyed on their own if you're feeling truly lazy! They also won't take you to the cleaners since they're all under $15 per bottle.

Wash 'n Wine Bar Picks
- Pighin Pinot Grigio—Italy
- Cloudy Bay Sauvignon Blanc—Australia
- Muga Rioja White—Spain
- Georges Dubœuf Beaujolais Nouveau—France

And if you want to splurge slightly, pop open this one for under $20:
- Domain Carneros Sparkling Wine—Spain

UNDERARM RX

Lots of the nonaccidental laundry gurus recommend dissolving 2–4 aspirin in a half cup of warm water, and letting the perspiration-stained underarm area soak in it for a few hours before washing. You can double or triple the dosage to cut down on the time. Regardless, it's a bit time-consuming, but if you have the time and the aspirin, take two and call me in the morning!

BURN THIS
Housewifely Calorie Counter

FEMALE: 125 lbs.

Moderately and continuously for 15 minutes

- Stretching: 35
- Lifting 10–20 lbs.: 57
- Ironing: 33
- Folding: 28

MALE: 165 lbs.

Moderately and continuously for 15 minutes

- Stretching: 47
- Lifting 10–20 lbs.: 75
- Ironing: 43
- Folding: 37

SOURCE: WWW.CALORIESPERHOUR.COM

B. DRYIN'

The Home Stretch

As they say in baseball, you're in the home stretch *and* it's the easiest stretch. All you need to master this cycle are the few basic dos and don'ts that follow. It's also where you'll need those fabric dryer sheets and tennis balls.

For those of you who are into laundry's toning benefits, this is another opportunity to *Tumble 'n Tone* as you choose.

Drying Dos and Don'ts

Dos

- Dry full loads (per machine capacity).
- Put in fabric softener sheet.
- Remove clothes immediately when cycle's done to help reduce wrinkling.

- Clean removable lint screen. Do so after every load to maintain efficiency.
- Do consecutive loads. It helps maintain the heat.
- *ONLY IF you're adventurous:* I have a few truly accidental friends who thaw large frozen food items in their dryer. Apparently, it acts like a convection oven. I haven't tried it, but if you do be sure to put the food on a dryer rack so it doesn't tumble. I've got to tell you, I'm not a fan of this idea, but my friends swear it works so I wanted to share it with you. However, if you do try this, to eliminate any chance of potential bacterial growth after thawing, I'd advise that you do the following:

- Be sure to cook all your foods thoroughly after thawing
- Sanitize your rack thoroughly in the dishwasher
- Liberally spray dryer with antibacterial disinfectant products
- Wipe dryer with antibacterial disinfectant cloths
- Consider buying a new dryer and use my friend's the next time you'd like to try this!

Don'ts

- Don't overload. It causes wrinkles, and therefore more ironing for Mama.
- Don't do partial loads. Full loads mean fewer loads and that means more free time. Plus it saves energy.
- Don't forget to check your care labels. Check fabric care and machine instructions. Refer to *Talk the Talk Laundry Care Guide* on page 48 if you're having trouble figuring out what to do.
- Don't drink too much. Have only one glass of wine since it may compromise your ironing.

For a little extra exercise, shake out laundry to help reduce wrinkling.

ANYONE FOR TENNIS?

Believe it or not, new tennis balls help fight static cling. They also help keep the poof in your pillows and comforters. So if you can stand the noise from them plopping about in your dryer, lob a few in!

C. IRONIN'

Boredom Is Thy Name

My second favorite household chore is ironing. My first being hitting my head on the top bunk bed until I faint.

—ERMA BOMBECK

Erma had it right, but it's not only a chore, it's a bore! Perhaps that's why they call the thing you do it on an ironing board—pardon the pun! The other reason it's so boring is that you can't really do anything else as you do it—forget the *Tumble 'n Tone* stuff, it could have your favorite shirt feeling a burn that will have you reeling. So what's an accidental housewife to do?

- Think positively: IT'S ALMOST OVER!!!
- Put on some headphones, listen to the radio, daydream, or do your hair—yes, I said your hair, but you'll have to read on to see what I'm talking about.

Stuff to Have Handy

- Downy Wrinkle Releaser
- Padded ironing board
- Steam iron with retractable cord
- Spray bottle with water

- Shower
- Curling iron
- Hair flattening or straightening iron
- Blow dryer
- OPTIONAL: Music or daydreams

Iron-Free Shortcuts

According to fashion industry experts, ironing is really not a good thing since it can ruin your clothes by taking the color out and hurting fibers. Clearly, I like the way they think. So for those of you who are like me and don't want to "risk" ruining your clothes by ironing them nor look like you slept in them, try these iron-free tips and shortcuts.

- SHAKE OUT BEFORE DRYING: Self-explanatory, *I hope.*
- DON'T OVERLOAD: Give your laundry enough room to tumble so it won't be crushed and wrinkle.
- DON'T PROCRASTINATE: Remove items immediately when the cycle's complete. If they're still damp and you have the room, put them on plastic hangers, and let them air-dry.
- THROW DRY STUFF INTO DRYER: This may sound odd, but by throwing sheets, linens, and lightweight clothing that have been sitting in the closet or drawer into the dryer with a damp towel, it will remove wrinkles.
- USE WRINKLE RELEASERS: Spray and stretch per instructions and you'll be good to go. For deeper wrinkles spray them and throw into the dryer on low. If you go the old-fashioned route and iron them, spraying deep wrinkles with water will also help.
- SHOWER AND STEAM: Put on plastic hangers in the bathroom while showering and let hang out.

- PURCHASE WRINKLE-FREE CLOTHING: Manufacturers realize that you don't want to do more work, so many of them are producing wrinkle-free and stain-repellant clothing and table linens. My son claims his wrinkle- and stain-free pants aren't as comfy as his regular pants. Seems the stuff they put on to help us do less work makes them a little stiffer. So what you gain in stain prevention you loose in comfort. Some of the companies making them are: Dockers, Eddie Bauer, Lands' End, LL Bean, The Gap, and Old Navy. And, believe it or not, even Brooks Brothers has wrinkle-free shirts and pants!

Hair Today, Wrinkle-Free Tomorrow

Almost every accidental housewife has at least one styling tool in their beauty and grooming arsenal to style their do. Thus, my friends, these wrinkle-free shortcuts are for you! They are recommended for minor, easy-to-reach wrinkles and not major ones or those hard-to-reach ones in the middle of your clothing. Check fabric care instructions before attempting and, if possible, try on small, remote section first. Please use good judgment and caution since these devices heat up pretty quickly.

- KNOW WHEN TO CURL THEM: For light wrinkles wrap article lightly around your hair curling iron and hold for a second or two. Repeat as needed. Do not try with plastic or any other synthetic material.
- FLATLINER: A hair flattening or straightening iron works like a mini press. Place slightly wrinkled area on flattening iron and hold for a second or two. Repeat as needed. Do not use on plastic or any other synthetic material.

- BLOW IT OUT: Your blow dryer is a wonderful tool to get wrinkles out of plastic tablecloths. Be careful not to overheat or it could also melt them.

AND Last . . .

If none of the preceding iron-free tips worked for you, there are five options left:

1. Iron (remember to check fabric care ironing instructions).
2. Send to dry cleaner.
3. Give to your mother to iron.
4. Fold them and blame wrinkles on drawer capacity.
5. Tell your boss you worked late, fell asleep and didn't have time to change.

Yo! You Done Good!

Way to go! You've learned the basics of laundry speak, the benefits of tumbling and toning, how to sort, pick the right varietal, *and* deal with PMS. I'd say that's quite an achievement, and one that hopefully will make this dirty cycle of your housewifely life easier and more bearable. Now, invite some friends over and chill some of those tasty wines you've got stored in your washing machine. I told you our species would find joy in housekeeping!

Task #3
ORGANIZING

FENG SHUI OUR WAY

Keeping my home organized isn't something I do either with pizzazz or with passion. I do have moments when I discard old magazines piled so high that they threaten my family's safety, toss clothes away that haven't seen the light of day for years, and chuck unopened mail that has a postmark older than my three-month-old pup, Woody. When I'm done, it feels *really* good. Truth is, I'm energized. But, these flourishes are few and far between. The real me loves to shift and straighten piles to make them look neat and write reminder notes to myself that I can never find. My brother Rick, a devotee of all things kung fu, took note of my organizational ways one day when I couldn't find my keys. He suggested I check out the teachings of feng shui (pronounced fung shway), the Chinese art of finding balance and harmony with our surroundings by placing things in a certain way to ease the flow of chi (energy) in our lives. Sounded great, until I realized that finding harmony with my surroundings by pointing all things north was not my way. But, achieving harmony by placing things in a certain way that suited my accidental organizational style was. So what follows is feng shui *our way*. As for easing the flow of chi, place a cup of coffee in your hand and point it toward your mouth. Facing north is optional.

THE ACCIDENTAL HOUSEWIFE'S ORGANIZATIONAL BASICS

Organizing is what you do before you do something so that when you do it, it's not all mixed up.

—Christopher Robin in *Winnie-the-Pooh*, by A.A. MILNE

Reality is that our hectic lifestyles do not always afford us the luxury of organizing things before we do something. And even if we did have the time, how we do it and where its place may be varies for each of us, which is why this task is a bit more challenging. Unlike cleaning, laundry, and meal planning (which follows), organizing isn't something that is easily accomplished with the aid of store-bought products or personal services. They can help, but only after you figure out what stays, what bills to pay, and what goes. That's why this section isn't organized like the others. It focuses first on what you'll need to think about instead of what stuff you'll need to get it done, so that your household isn't "all mixed up."

Numero Uno Organizing Rule: *Control "It"!*

Clutter seems to mount with reckless abandon, and just when you think you've got some of it under control it returns with a vengeance. "It" can also be very deceiving. Many of us don't even know what "it" is since clutter can easily blend into our decor, be stashed away, or ignored. But facts are facts, and eventually you have to get "it" under control. Here's how:

1. Know and identify what "it" is.
2. Ask key questions to help you reduce "it."

3. Find the right places for "it" at home or elsewhere that suits your accidental style.

Simple enough, *so let's get to "it."*

What's Your Organizational Style?

You may think that because you're disorganized or disinterested that you don't have an organizational style, but you do. For example, I've already admitted that my way of dealing with clutter is to shift and straighten. Since I realized this, it hasn't changed my ways dramatically, but it has resulted in an occasional toss, shift, and straighten— toss being the operative word here, since it means I'm cutting *some* clutter. That's why I thought it might be useful for you to try to identify what type of organizer you are before moving on to the how-tos. Perhaps, like me, by knowing how you consciously or unconsciously deal with clutter you may cut some without advance planning. Obviously I'm no shrink, so the descriptions that follow are not based on clinical observation, but rather on instincts, personal observations, and input from fellow accidental housewives. It's also possible you may discover that you have traits found in more than one of those described. Fear not, this is a rather common condition found among accidental types!

Which One Are You?

- THE STUFFER: Stuffs (i.e., puts) everything into a concealed space such as a drawer, under a bed, or into a closet. Your type does not eliminate or organize until spaces are stuck, overflowing, become a fire hazard, or result in missed appointments and relentless calls from bill collectors.
- THE SHIFTER: Moves things such as mail, magazines, shoes, pho-

tographs, and eyeglasses from one place to another and straightens the shifted pile to make it appear neat and organized. Shifting into the garbage, recycling, or donating occurs only when obvious harm can befall a household member due to the pile's ability to topple and crush.

- THE SCHMEARER: Is drawn to large open areas such as countertops, tub rims, end tables, desks, or entranceways, which enable you to indulge your affinity to schmear (i.e., spread) things around. These things include: mail, magazines, newspapers, shoes, and loose change. Action is taken only when there is no space left for your morning cup of coffee or room to schmear your bagel.
- THE HOARDER: Has never met an item, piece of mail, or gift that you didn't like. You collect everything and suffer from acute separation anxiety anytime someone mentions parting with a "hoarded" item. You react to the overflow only when your significant other or a family member is displaced as a result of its location. You believe that by relocating your stuff from a countertop to a storage box under your bed means that you have become more organized.
- THE DAWDLER: Is found in all of us. Whether you stuff, shift, schmear, or hoard you're engaging in a form of dawdling (i.e., procrastinating). It may be a means of avoidance, fear of separation, or just laziness, but it's still dawdling and you're not dealing with your household chaos or clutter.

P.O.T.T.Y. Training 101: Finding Harmony with Your Space

In all chaos there is a cosmos, in all disorder a secret order.

—CARL JUNG

Now there's a guy who either truly understood the mind-set of an accidental housewife, was one himself, or both. So with Mr. Jung's words

WHAT'S YOUR HOUSEHOLD ORGANIZATIONAL HI Q?

What or who is feng shui?

1. A Chinese noodle dish

2. A rare dog breed

3. Wind and water

4. A well-known Ming Dynasty philosopher

5. Julie's dry cleaner

What is the most common expression voiced when organizing?

1. Am I done yet?

2. Oh, that's where that is!"*

3. Is this really mine?

4. Help!

5. Time flies when you're having fun!

Source: Barry Zelick, National Organization of Professional Organizers

Which of the following do not have an expiration date?

1. Prescriptions/Medications

2. Condoms

3. Makeup

4. Wine

What is not an advisable place to place/store condoms?

1. Your wallet

2. Back pocket

3. Night table

4. Photo tree

5. Lights

ANSWERS 3, 2, 4, 5

in mind it's time to get to the task and learn how to control our clutter by engaging in **P.O.T.T.Y. Training 101**—Personal Organizing Targets, Tips, and Yoga. Specifically, you'll learn how to identify clutter culprits, where they live, and what questions to ask yourself to help cut it. You'll also be introduced to some simple Yoga techniques should you wish to find harmony with your body and mind as well as with your surroundings.

Know Your Target

These three words sort of go along with the theory "I'll know it when I see it." Of course, as I mentioned in the beginning of this task, that means you need to know what "it" is. To make this easier, I've broken this section into two categories: *What "It" May Be* and *Where You Might Find "It."* Please note that *these lists are provided as a guide and are not all-encompassing.*

What "It" May Be:
- Mail
- Magazines, newspapers, and catalogs
- Business cards
- Notes to self
- Photographs
- Shopping bags
- Shoes
- Kids' memorabilia (artwork, report cards, papers, first teeth, etc.)
- Miscellaneous stuff (change, buttons, matches, pens, etc.)

Where You Might Find "It":
- Closets
- Counters
- Drawers

- Dressers
- Entranceways
- Pantries and cabinets
- Tub rims
- Under beds

NOTE: Since I don't want to overwhelm you with too much info, home offices, garages, attics, and cars are not included. However, many of the ideas suggested can be applied easily to organizing these areas should you get the urge.

Keep "It" Focused

The objective of all our tasks is to keep them short, easy, and efficient. You don't want to overdo your efforts nor lose your sanity by taking on more than you can handle. Here's how you can make the organizational process relatively swift and painless:

- *Select One Target:* You choose, but pick *only one* type of clutter (i.e., mail, magazines, photographs) or one place (i.e., closets, entranceways, countertops) where you are likely to find clutter and focus on it. This will help you have a beginning and an end that is manageable and achievable.
- *Avoid Distractions:* No cell phone, no TV, no friends stopping by, no food in the oven or appointments to keep.
- *Do It When You're In the Mood:* As in all our housewifely tasks, don't do it if you're not in the mood since you'll be resentful, probably rush through it, or throw something important away. The good thing about organizing is that since there are so many different types of tasks you can do, you can select one that works with your mood or how much time you have. So, if all you have is five minutes, select something that you can do from start to finish within that time.

By the way, you'll be surprised at how many things you can actually do in five minutes. Check out *Take Five and Organize!* on page 116 to learn more.

· *Stay Relaxed:* For most of us, organizing is boring. As a result, it's easy to become overwhelmed and want to stop almost as soon as we start. That's where knowing how to relax comes into play and why I've come to value the use of Yoga as a good relaxation technique for this task. You may already know the virtues of Yoga and be able to blend it in on your own, but for those who are new to Yoga, the following personal tale, breathing exercises, and poses may help you to stay focused and relaxed from beginning to end.

AN ACCIDENTAL ASIDE

Hey, Hey, Hey, It's Yogi Julie!

I must confess that before writing this book, I knew little to nothing about Yoga other than my impression that it was nontaxing and for those who weren't really into a major workout. But after years of hearing Marla, my best bud and a die-hard Yoga fanatic, rave about its calming and toning effects, it dawned on me that it might help with this task. Marla was thrilled and put me in touch with John Tunney, a true Yoga master and the owner of www.yogasite.com. I explained to John that I wasn't a believer, but that Marla thought Yoga and organizing might be a good fit. He agreed. John was kind enough to put together a few relaxation and focusing exercises for me to try that required no previous training. And, I must admit, after using them to get me through my closet organizing, I am a believer. In fact I've become a Yogi, which is what they call folks who practice Yoga. So, what follows is Yoga Your Way. It's just enough Yoga to get you relaxed and focused as you begin organizing, keep you steady when you're about to lose it, and revive you when you're done.

NOTE: Due to the relaxing nature of the exercises, it is possible that you may doze off in the beginning, middle, or end. Just resume where you left off when you awake! Playing spa-like music and lighting scented candles are recommended by yours truly, Yogi Julie.

YOGA YOUR WAY

STARTING: *The Yogic Breath.* John says that this is a good way to focus on the task ahead, since it will clear your head as you relax your mind and body. Here's how you do it:

- Sit in a chair, on a cushion, or on the floor with your back straight near the targeted organizing item or place.
- Close your eyes and breathe through your nose.
- Focus on your breath.
  - Draw it into your belly and let your tummy fill with air like a balloon.
  - Continue to inhale and let your lower ribs expand as you draw your breath into your lungs.
  - Continue to inhale and fill the upper lungs with air.
  - Exhale slowly and reverse the procedure.
  - Repeat several times.

You're now ready to focus and do it!

MIDWAY BOOST: *The Sun Breath.* According to John, this will help you when you're about to lose it. Breathing and movement will energize your body, release tension, and calm your mind. Love that!

- Stand with your feet about hip-width apart.
- Inhale through your nose for a count of four while bringing your hands into prayer position at your heart.

- Lift your arms out first to your sides and then sweep them up toward the ceiling until the back of your hands touch.
- Gently arch your back and lift your chin slightly.
- Look up at your hands.
- Exhale, separate your hands, and let your arms float down to your sides.
- Bring your hands back into prayer position at chest level.
- Repeat 3–5 times.

OR

Until your prayers are answered or your desire to continue is restored!

FINITO RE-VIVE: *The Corpse or Savasana Pose.* At the end of your organizing bout you may be feeling mentally and physically drained. John recommends this posture since he claims it will help you relax, release tension and stress, and restore vitality.

- Lie on your back on the floor (you can use a mat or blanket), feet slightly apart, arms at sides with palms facing up. Do not lie on your bed or couch since you are likely to go to sleep. Pillows are OK.
- Close your eyes and take several deep breaths.
- Let your bod soften and sink into the floor.
- Focus your breath on one area at a time such as your feet.
  - Inhale, exhale, and relax your feet.
- Repeat with each part of your body. Move up to your legs, hips, stomach, chest, back, shoulders, arms, neck, and face.
- When you reach the top (i.e., your head) focus on your breath and watch it move in and out. Truly a *must-see!*
- Roll over to one side and slowly sit up.
  (Stay seated a few moments before standing or taking that snooze you've been dying for!)

If you'd like to learn more relaxing breaths and postures visit John's site at www.yogasite.com.

Keep "It" or Cut "It"

Regardless of whether you're The Stuffer, The Shifter, The Schmearer, The Hoarder, or The Dawdler, it will be helpful in your "cutting" endeavors to ask yourself the following questions:

1. Is It Time-Sensitive?

Will *not* dealing with your clutter result in loss of home, friends, quiet nights, or money? Categories include but are not limited to bills, invitations, reminder notes about appointments, condoms, warranties, and lottery tickets.

2. Does It Exceed Height and Space Limits?

Have things accumulated to the point where they are more than a foot high and could cause injury or damage? Categories include but are not limited to newspapers, magazines, catalogs, garbage, junk mail, shoes, laundry (See Task #2), and bottles of wine.

3. Is It Really Worth Saving?

Does it have sentimental value or serve a purpose? Categories include but are not limited to photographs, phone numbers, shopping bags, the outfit you wore on your first date with your significant other, kids' stuff including everything from their favorite toy or stuffed animal from years gone by, to first teeth (all of them!), report cards, artwork, and so on.

BURN THIS
Housewifely Calorie Counter

FEMALE: 125 lbs.

Moderately and continuously for 30 minutes

- Packing: 99
- Yoga: 71
- Sexual activity*: 60

MALE: 165 lbs.

Moderately and continuously for 30 minutes

- Packing: 131
- Yoga: 94
- Sexual activity*: 79

* based on accidental housewifely average of 15 minutes

SOURCE: WWW.CALORIESPERHOUR.COM

4. Does It Deserve a Better Life?

Are the dishes in your cabinets so dusty that you could write your take-out order on them? Categories include but are not limited to clothing, shoes, sets of dishes, coffee mugs, picture frames, toys, unopened gifts from housewarmings, birthdays, weddings, anniversaries, etc.

By the way, if this question gave you cause to wonder, the likelihood is the answer is yes! So be kind and find "it" a new home!

EVERYTHING HAS ITS PLACE

Women need a reason to have sex—men just need a place.

—BILLY CRYSTAL

I know this task requires you to digest and sort through a lot, so you may feel a bit overwhelmed. But by the end of this chapter you'll feel energized and most things in your home that you care about *will* find a place that works for you! This section offers place-saving solutions for those things and suggests items that will help keep them organized. I've also included an occasional idea for discarding items, but the detailed list of how and where to get rid of this stuff is in Good Rid'ins on page 110.

The Stuff You're Gonna Need

As I mentioned earlier, unlike cleaning, laundry, and mealtime (which follows), there aren't many store-bought products available for this task that can help across the board. But what follows are those that will aid you at least with the basic sorting and storing. Per usual, a few excessities are listed, too! A Personal Organizing Resources list to help you locate these items is found on page 109.

FYI: *The Place-Saving Shopping List* is available in a downloadable version on my website, www.theaccidentalhousewife.com. It also includes all the items suggested throughout Place-Saving Solutions so you can check off what you'll need once you decide which ideas work for you.

The Place-Saving Shopping List

Necessities:
- Stuffing and Organizing containers:
  - Baskets (colors and sizes are your call)
  - Clear plastic boxes with covers (so you can see contents)
  - Large plastic garbage bags
- Ziploc plastic bags with preset writing spaces
- Color-coded labels or Brother P-Touch electronic labeler
- Permanent marker pens

Excessities (As noted earlier, these go particularly well with the Yoga exercises!)
- Scented candles or calming incense oils or sticks
- Spa-like relaxation music

SIMPLE ORGANIZING IDEAS
with Stuff You Might Already Have Handy

- **HATS WITH BRIM:** Coins or keys.
- **CORKS:** Use as jewelry pin cushion, key chain holder.
- **GOLF BAG AND CLUBS:** Hang hats and umbrellas.
- **GOLF TEES:** Stick in piece of foam and use for rings, link jewelry, hoop earrings, etc.
- **GLOVE WIDOWS:** Stuff with plastic from dry cleaner and use to organize watches, rings, bracelets.
- **HAIR CLIPS:** Filing aid for paper stuff including bills, menus, notes, biz cards, etc.
- **ICE BUCKET:** Keep brushes, curling irons, change; or hang eyeglasses on side.
- **NAIL POLISH:** Use to color-code keys, hooks. A second coat may be required.
- **SOAP BARS:** Use golf tees, insert toothpick or olive picks to hang chains or rings. Keep away from sinks and candles.
- **PHOTOGRAPHS:** Use dupes to ID organizing spaces.
- **STUFFED ANIMALS:** Use as pin cushion; eyeglass or hair clip holder.
- **TOOTHBRUSH HOLDER:** Put in pencils, pens, eyeliners, lip liners, anything thin and straight.

Place-Saving Solutions

Place-Saving Solutions are listed alphabetically by item or area for easy reference and spontaneous organizing romps. If something's missing, feel free to let me know on my website at www.theaccidentalhousewife .com. I'll do my best to help you find "it" a place. It's also a really good idea and time-saver to keep extra Ziploc bags, containers, labels, and markers near items and areas you know are your biggest clutter spots so you can "cut" on a whim.

AN ACCIDENTAL ASIDE

Mind over Matter

As noted, feng shui is rooted in the belief that clutter obstructs our ability to find harmony with our surroundings and the flow of energy (chi) around us. This led me to ponder the effects it might have inside the bedroom. I for one have lots of trouble sleeping and wondered if the stuff on my night table or under my bed might be keeping me up. Then a friend shared that she and her hubs were experiencing difficulties keeping or getting it up during moments of passion. Was this a coincidence or was the clutter in our bedrooms responsible for both our dilemmas? I just had to know, so I told her about feng shui and she was as eager as I to clear her bedroom clutter. A few weeks later the results were in: Harmony was restored to all. I was (and am) sleeping through the night and the energy flow betwixt my friend and her husband improved significantly. Mind over matter? I don't know, but if it works, who cares!

Baseball Hats (also see Change and Keys)

Chuck any hats that are permanently discolored, stretched, smell, or have been in the same place for over three months. For the ones you want to keep here are a variety of ideas:

- Buy an expandable coffee mug rack and hang on back of door closest to the most-used entrances or exits.
- Get a decorative floor-standing coatrack.
- Knot a rope, piece of twine, or necktie to a hook on the back of

closet door and attach colorful clothes clips. Color-code to keep ownership straight.

- Hang a pix of household members above hooks on closet door or entranceway wall.
- Store sentimental faves in plastic storage boxes or create a display.

Alternatively:
- Give to friends or family suffering from male-pattern baldness.

Change

Place in multiple and strategic locations: kitchen, bedroom closet, dresser, car.

Collect in:
- Piggy bank
- Small bowl
- Plastic bags
- Unused baseball caps

Alternatively:
- Start a fund for cosmetic surgery, hairpiece, or pampering indulgence of choice.

Clothing

Empty everything from closet or drawers onto clean floor, bed, or couch. Have bags or cartons labeled CHUCK, STORE, or DONATE and begin. It's up to you if you want to get more specific and list the contents. Judge keepers by use, size, and if wearing them says "loser," then

- Organize by type: shirts, pants, skirts, jackets, suits, etc.
- Save space by rolling T-shirts up vs. folding.

- Put sweaters in plastic boxes under bed or keep in closet.
- Use a shoe bag for socks, belts, briefs, bras, and oh yeah, shoes, too!

Alternatively:
- Call closet organizer.
- Re-gift new, unworn items.

Condoms/Protective-Enhancing Stuff

Two things to think about:

1. EXPIRATION DATES: Yes, even these have them, so check before using or you may soon be checking diapers instead.
2. EASY ACCESS: They're only good if you have them handy. Here are a few places to help you do just that:
   - Bedroom night table
   - Purse
   - Pill box
   - Wallet

Condoms Only:
- Keep in back pocket *(Please note that if you leave them in your pants pocket and wash them, throw them away.)*
- Clip onto photo tree
- Attach to lampshades with hair clips, paper clips, or clothespins. *Do not use safety pins as they might pierce the condoms.*

FYI: My male experts tell me that you should never keep condoms near any heat source since it can affect their effectiveness, so be sure lights are out or that they are far away from anything that gives off heat other than your body.

Cosmetics/Makeup

I decided to reach out for help on these items since they bring out The Hoarder in me, and I suspect I am not alone. Over the years, I have assembled an impressive collection of partially used eye shadows, eyeliners, lip pencils, blushes, and lipsticks. The problem is that most of them have not seen the light of day for months or even years since I have replaced them with what I think are this season's must-haves. Needing room, and not quite ready to part with last season's musts, I usually put them all in one plastic bag under my bathroom sink "just in case" I need that special blue liner. That's why for this place-saving category, I decided to seek professional help, and there was only one person to go to—the amazing and esteemed cosmetic guru, my dear friend and a fellow accidental housewife (except when it comes to this!), Bobbi Brown! As you can imagine, Bobbi was far from surprised at my hoardish ways and quickly reassured me that indeed, I was not alone. In fact, she was delighted to help us and to share timely tips and simple ways we can cut some of our cosmetic clutter. Here's how:

BOBBI BROWN'S COSMETIC CLUTTER CUTTERS:

HOW TO FIGURE OUT WHAT STAYS AND WHAT GOES
The easiest way to do this is to dump out all the contents in your makeup drawer or bag and create three piles:

1. TRASH: Take anything that's broken, smells funny, or has changed color and immediately trash it.
2. GIVEAWAY: Group together anything that has not expired and is unopened and put it in a box to give to a women's shelter, your local high school drama department, your daughter, or a niece for when she wants to play dress-up.

BOBBI BROWN'S 5–10 MINUTE FACE-SAVING MAKEUP TIPS

Bobbi's too kind a person to ever refer to the way we look in the morning as unattractive, since she sees only the beauty in all of us. I, however, like so many of us, tend to see the beast in me as I look in the mirror before my first cup of morning coffee and my housewifely life beckons. It is then, as I prepare to drive my son to school, that I reach for my sunglasses to hide from the world. But help is on the way! Bobbi's got some simple ways to organize our look so that we can face the world without dark glasses when speed and need are the order of our day.

5-MINUTE FACE-SAVING MAKEUP LOOK

This is the makeup routine you go for when you're tight on time and don't want to look like you just rolled out of bed. It's a low-key look that's perfect when you're taking the kids to school, running errands, or going to the gym.

- Use creamy concealer under eyes to cover dark circles.
- Apply stick foundation or tinted moisturizer around the nose where there's redness.
- Put on a coat of brown or black mascara if you're fair. If you're one of the lucky ones and have dark lashes you can skip this!
- Apply cream blush stick on the apples of cheeks.
- Complete with lip balm or tinted lip gloss—color is up to you!

10-MINUTE FACE-SAVING MAKEUP LOOK

Ten minutes is all you need to create a polished and pulled-together look that can go from the office to luncheons and other daytime events. It's a full face of makeup, but it's quick, so you won't have to get up at the crack of dawn.

- Use creamy concealer on dark circles. It instantly brightens your face.
- Apply foundation all over face.
- Set concealer with sheer face powder for a smooth look that lasts.
- Shape and define brows with eye shadow toned to your natural hair color; use an eyebrow brush for the most natural look.
- Use a light eye shadow all over your upper lid, medium eye shadow on the lower lid, and a dark eye shadow for the liner.
- Apply one or two coats of black mascara.
- Use a neutral blush layered with a brighter shade of blush for a pop of color.
- Pull it all together with a lipstick and gloss.

You're now ready to face your accidental life with or without sunglasses!

3. WHAT'S LEFT: Use a critical and honest eye to ask yourself:
- Are there a handful of products that I always reach for?
- Do I have multiples of a shade or formula?
- What colors make me feel the prettiest?
- How long have I had it?

Which leads us to the following:

Like food, even makeup has a shelf life. So before bacteria start to set up shop in your favorite lipstick, here's a guide to how long you can expect your makeup to stay fresh:

- Face powder and powder blush: 2 years
- Foundation: 1–1½ years
- Lipstick: 1–1½ years
- Moisturizer: 1–1½ years
- Lip and eye pencils: 1 year
- Eye shadow: 1 year

- Eye cream: 1 year
- Cream blush: 6 months to 1 year
- Mascara: 3–6 months

Now, go and cut some of your cosmetic clutter!

Here are some place-saving solutions that Bobbi and I came up with for "what's left":

For your everyday keepers, keep handy in:
- Small zippered cosmetic bag or Ziploc bags (also great for traveling!)
- Plastic utensil divider
- Tiered cosmetic, art supply, or fishing tackle box
- Space-saving, tiered lazy Susan

  TIP: Group lip liners and eye pencils together with rubber bands.

For occasional/seasonal keepers:
- Store in individual Ziploc bags and label by season (fall, winter, spring, or summer) or type (lipsticks, eyeliners, eye shadows, etc.).

  TIP: Keep nearby for when a special occasion, the season, or your mood changes.

For brushes, be decorative and use:
- Small vase (be sure bottom is wider than top so it doesn't tilt)
- Coffee mug or
- Multiple toothbrush holder

Alternatively for old stuff:
- Use to decorate pumpkins, clay pots, etc.

You should also check with your favorite makeup line to see what kinds of organizers they have, since they've realized your passion for fashion even when it comes to storing makeup and brushes.

For makeup and beauty tips, and to learn what's new and more about this amazing entrepreneur, accidental housewife, and mom, visit Bobbi's site at www.bobbibrowncosmetics.com.

Entryway Stuff

Here are a bunch of ideas:

- Hang a shoe bag on back of entranceway door for sunscreen, sunglasses, gloves, scarves, knit hats.
- Put appropriate photos or large decorative initials above designated hooks on closet doors or shoe cubbies to create personal zones for stuff like hats, coats, umbrellas, footwear, etc.
- Place large color-coded plastic buckets or baskets near entranceways to identify where each household member should toss their shoes rather than having them scattered all over the floor.
- Buy a decorative standing coatrack.
- Recycle an old golf bag; leave in a few clubs for hanging stuff like hats, scarves, umbrellas, and dog leashes.
- Put hooks up for keys or have unbreakable dish nearby (see *Keys*).

Eyeglasses

Try to put them near places you use them most, like the TV area, bathroom, kitchen, near the main phone, or on your face! If you wear them just for reading, consider buying cheap extras. It's worth the little extra clutter it may cause to be able to find them easily.

- Hang on hooks or cabinet handles near areas where you use them most (kitchen near phone or countertop).
- Purchase photo tree holders to hang them on, folded.

- Buy decorative eyeglass holders that look and are shaped like noses.
- Put a large rubber band around a coffee mug or small clay pot and "hook" 'em on.
- Lay them unfolded on a stuffed animal.

Hairbrushes, combs, curling irons

Collect them in:

- Baskets
- Lazy Susan
- Ice bucket
- Tool belt
- Fabric-covered jewelry box

Medications

Check expiration dates. Flush or chuck unused or old prescriptions. Store your medications separately from your children's and pets'. The following may also help:

- Buy pill separators.
- Use color-coded rings—available at Target stores.

Alternatively:
- Ask your local pharmacist if they'll get rid of them for you.
- Go into drug rehab.

Jewelry

There are lots of places to keep your jewelry and watches, so when you consider any of the places below, keep the following in mind:

- Access: Keep the stuff you wear most often in places you can get to them easiest.
- Fragility: Keep stuff that can scratch easily or is fragile, like silver, pearls, and watches, separate unless you can afford to replace them at whim.
- Visibility: Don't keep the good stuff in plain sight for everyone to see.

For individual stuff:

- Necklaces and bracelets: Hang on hooks or coffee mug rack. For thin, chain-dangling stuff: Hang on corkboard using pushpins to secure.
- Earrings and rings: Place in jumbo egg cartons or ice cube trays.
- Pins: Use decorative small pillows, pin cushions, ice cube trays, egg cartons, or foam rubber.
- Silver: It tarnishes, so buy tarnish-free jewelry pouches.
- Fine chain jewelry: Use straws. Cut to size, drop through and fasten.

Alternatively:

- Hope diamond: Put in safe deposit box or bury in backyard beyond Fido's sniffing zones.

All-purpose organizers:

- Plastic dividers for flatware
- Drawer dividers
- Small boxes that fit into drawer
- Sectional serving trays/dishes
- Tackle, art, or decorative jewelry boxes
- Metal-parts cabinets
- Use an old glove stuffed with plastic from your dry cleaning for rings, bracelets, pins, and watches
- Give to relatives with little or no taste

AN ACCIDENTAL ASIDE

Counter Intelligence

I don't know about you, but when I wash dishes I like to take off my rings—particularly my engagement ring. I always used to put it on a very pretty and colorful spoon rest. Well, a few years ago my husband and I had just moved into our new home where the countertops were granite—the marbleized kind—and my spoon rest was still sitting in a yet to be unpacked carton. Too lazy to put my engagement ring in a safe place, I put it on a white napkin far from the sink. That was my first and last mistake. When I went to put it back on I quickly realized that the napkin was missing, as was my engagement ring. Frantically, I emptied all the garbage in our kitchen sink onto the floor, then had my husband open the sink's drainpipe, searched the floors, nooks, and crannies but unfortunately came up empty-handed. My ring was gone. So the moral of this story is:

- Always put your rings or other fine jewelry in a highly visible but secure place (ring box, cabinet, bedroom, but no place near or above the kitchen or any sink).
- Keep your insurance up to date: Generally precious gems and stones appreciate, so they're worth more now than they were when you bought them. That doesn't mean you should take the next opportunity to flush them down the toilet or sink—insurance folks are very thorough and not very trusting of accidents of this sort.

Keys

Unless you're 100 percent sure that you'll never figure out what some keys are for, it's a good idea to save them in a plastic bag and store.

Who knows, you may discover they unlock a safety deposit box with valuable stuff! Keep those that are used every day near entrances and exits. For keepers:

- Toss into a small unbreakable bowl.
- Hang on hooks below pictures of household members.
- Color-code key chains with tape or nail polish. Hang on hooks, small knobs on entranceway drawer, counter, or hanging coffee mug rack.
- Collect in a straw hat from last vacation or baseball cap.
- Put golf tees in piece of foam rubber or cork. Use marker to color-code different sets and who they belong to.

Alternatively:

- Invest in an electronic key locator available at www.sharperimage .com, brookstone.com, and other similar techie-type stores.
- Get keyless entry system installed.

Kids' Memorabilia

The last thing you want to do is chuck something that your little ones believe to be a masterpiece or a memento of a monumental moment in their lives. On the other hand, by the time they reach puberty they'll have forgotten about all of this stuff unless they're an aspiring Picasso or Mary Higgins Clark. Bottom line is, you can't keep everything, so here are a few ideas to preserve their evolving self-esteem and your attempts to establish some order:

For teeth:

- After the first one, they all look the same, and kids just want the Tooth Fairy to pay them for their loss. So save the first in a small store-bought box, pouch, or plastic bag and be sure to date it. Anyway, by the time they're in braces they'll hate their teeth, and won't even care about nor remember their first one.

For artwork:

- Frame the art they're passionate about or hang it on a wall in their playroom or
- Depending on size: Roll it up in tubes found in the center of wrapping paper or paper towel rolls.

For report cards:

- Put in plastic sleeves and keep in a large photo album along with class pictures.

For tests and other stuff:

- Put in a box and have your kids decorate it or keep in a "special" dated notebook.

Paper Stuff (Mail, Magazines, Newspapers, Business Cards, etc.)

This category is probably one of the biggest clutter offenders, so finding places for it isn't always easy. But here are a few ideas and a simple sorting and recycling tip: Always keep a bag handy near the area where you open, read, or use this stuff so you can chuck anytime!

BILLS

Best strategy is to open them immediately. Otherwise, create a designated and *highly visible* place (refrigerator door, kitchen counter, near where you keep wallet or keys, etc.) to organize them, such as:

- Napkin holder
- Notebook labeled MUST PAY TO STAY
- Envelope labeled MUST PAY attached with magnets to fridge
- Corkboard near most-used phone

Alternatively:

- Pay electronically.

BUSINESS/APPOINTMENT CARDS AND PHONE NUMBERS

Chuck and recycle any that you can't remember where or from whom they came or if appointment date has passed. Put keepers in:

- Rolodex-type system
- Small basket or bowl
- Computer or electronic handheld organizer

COUPONS

Check expiration dates. Put in wallet, on fridge, or anyplace you'll see them and remember to use them. Chuck if expired.

JUNK MAIL (INCLUDES CATALOGS)

It's called junk mail for a reason—*It's Junk!* Therefore chuck and recycle it immediately upon receipt. You can be sure you'll see the same things again soon even if the catalog's cover photo changes.

NEWSPAPERS AND MAGAZINES

Cancel subscriptions if you haven't looked at them for three months or more. By then your "newspapers" will be "oldpapers" anyway. Otherwise:

- Roll and store in wine racks.
- Toss into baskets.
- Use for gift wrap.
- Have a bonfire.
- Recycle.

NOTES TO SELF

Put chalkboard or corkboard with pushpins and note paper near areas where you'll actually see them.

Photographs

First thing to do is dump dupes then:
- Personally or professionally transfer to video or DVD
- Put into A to Z recipe boxes or binders with plastic sheets or
- Label and store in plastic boxes.

Alternatively:
- Use as postcards.
- Create collage for gift wrap.
- Throw a filing party with friends.

Recipes

Who are you kidding! If you haven't tried them and they've been sitting around for a while, chuck 'em! If you still can't part with them and have visions of Martha grandeur, put them in a coated, three-ring binder with plastic sheets or good ole-fashioned card file. Alphabetize if possible!

Shoes

Chuck or donate if they have holes, haven't been worn in over a year, are seriously out of date, or kill your feet. Keep keepers in/on:

- Shoe bag
- Shoe rack or shoe tree
- Shoe boxes
- Plastic bins or baskets near entranceways
- Sturdy coatrack
- Heavy-duty large pegs or coffee mug rack hung in closet

Shopping Bags

These accumulate almost as quickly as the *Paper Stuff,* so you need an equally quick and painless exit strategy for them. Here are some perfect places, uses, and clutter-cutting ways to get rid of them:

- Use as gift bags.
- Keep in closet for easy "dumping" of clothes, shoes, or other items you want to give away.
- Use as the container for other recyclable stuff (newspapers, magazines, junk mail, etc.) or garbage.
- Use for disposable stuff and kids' toys for travel.
- Store miscellaneous toys.

Alternatively:
- Store in gaps between cabinets and walls.

Socks and Stockings

Keep them rolled up and housed in:

- shoe bag.
- empty tennis ball can.
- jumbo-size egg carton.

Ties

Name one guy who doesn't have at least a dozen ties they've never worn and I'll eat 'em!

First thing is to sort and abort by:
- Last time they saw light of day
- If they're in style

- Your/his affection for them
- If you'll hurt anyone's feelings by tossing

Then, keep 'em tidy:
- Roll neatly and place in shoe bag
- Hang on:
  - Electronic tie racks
  - Hangers
  - Coffee mug racks
  - Hooks
  - Doorknobs (could even hang some knobs in or outside of the closet and make your wall decorative!)

Alternatively:
- Re-gift those in style.
- Tie on to cabinet handle and use to hang glasses.

Toilet Paper

Keep within arm's reach.

- Stack several on a paper-towel holder.
- Put a bunch in nearby basket.

Alternatively:
- Eat less fiber.
- Drink less water.

Take-out Menus

Chuck duplicates and those unused for more than six months.

- Post on cork or Peg-Board near kitchen phone.
- Clip together with hair clips, decorative clothespins, or paper clips.

- Put in 3-ring binder with plastic sleeves.
- Store in accordion, alphabetized folder.

Alternatively:
- Cook (who am I kidding?!).
- Eat out.
- Go on diet.

Toys, Games, and Stuffed Animals

Practice the "one in, one out" rule when you or your little ones receive something new. For the "outs" let the little ones select a charity they'd like to give a donation to. The keepers can go in plastic rolling crates, see-through storage boxes, baskets, oversize buckets, or bins. Put a key word like "games" or pix on outside to help identify what's in them and keep organized.

For miscellaneous items use:
- Ziploc bags for small cars, game pieces, etc.
- Shoe bags
- Shopping bags (labelled)

TIP: For organizing LEGOS check out Box4blox.com.

Wine

Now we're talking! Remember to keep those with corks on their sides. But check, 'cause the trend is toward screw-tops, which are an accidental dream innovation come true!

Store in:
- Decorative wine racks
- Oven (only if its only function is as a decorative piece in your kitchen)
- Wooden crates

Alternatively:
- Re-gift
- Host a wine-tasting party

PERSONAL ORGANIZING RESOURCES

Here are some national stores and resources to help you find some of the organizing stuff mentioned throughout Everything Has Its Place. A few personal organizer resources are also included.

Personalized Resources:
- California Closets: www.calclosets.com. Offers complimentary consultation.
- Closet Factory: www.closetfactory.com.
- The Container Store: www.thecontainerstore.com.
- NAPO: www.napo.com. National Association of Professional Organizers has a list of its members by location and the kinds of organizing they specialize in, so see which is right for you.

Place-Saving and Organizing-Stuff Resources:
- Bed Bath & Beyond: www.bedbathandbeyond.com
- Crate & Barrel: www.crateandbarrel.com
- Hold Everything: www.holdeverything.com
- Ikea: www.ikea.com
- Lillian Vernon (catalog and Web site only—they have "store and organizational" tab on site): www.lillianvernon.com

- Linens 'n Things: www.lnt.com
- Pottery Barn: www.potterybarn.com
- Restoration Hardware: www.restorationhardware.com
- Stacks and Stacks (catalog and website, only): www.stacksand stacks.com
- Target (they have "organizational" tab on site): www.target.com
- The Container Store: www.containerstore.com

GOOD RID'INS

OK, you've made the big decision as to what stays, and you've learned some place-saving solutions for that stuff. Now it's time to figure out how to get rid of the stuff you don't want. I understand this may be difficult for some of you, particularly for The Hoarder. Just keep reminding yourself that by donating or simply giving it away you're doing a *really good deed*—you're helping people! And, look on the bright side—you're freeing up space so you can collect some brand-new clutter!

So here we go:

To simplify things I've divided the Good Rid'ins strategies into three parts. The first gives you the easiest rid techniques, while the second and third suggest good (and reliable) places to get rid of your stuff internationally, nationally, and locally.

Top Rid Strategies

Please note: The following are listed alphabetically and not in order of their effectiveness—that will depend on your organizational style, interest, and the amount of money you find. You can:

- Chuck.
- Donate.

- Hire personal organizer or clutter-buster services.
- Light bonfire.
- Plan garage sale.
- Re-gift.
- Sell online.

Procrastinators' Notice

The fourth week in March is National Clutter Awareness Week. So, if you're The Dawdler you can always put organizing off until then. Unfortunately, I'll be on vacation that week, so I'll catch up with all upon my return.

Easy Rid National 'n International Resources

This is by no means an all-inclusive list. It is a partial list with some overlap that will provide you with enough national and international services, charities, and organizations to help you start finding a proper home for some of your excess stuff. Another option is to go online and search for resources in your area by using key words such as "clothing donations (your state)." You should also check out charities that match your personal interests and causes, since there are so many good ones that need your stuff. And, if you aren't so sure who's reputable or not, go to www.charitynavigator.org which lists more than 4,000 charities.

CLOTHING, ACCESSORIES, MAKEUP, BABY STUFF, DISHES, ETC.

1. GOODWILL: www.goodwill.org. They accept new or gently used items like clothing, appliances, and furniture and sell them in their 3,000 retail store locations throughout North America.
2. SALVATION ARMY: www.salvationarmyusa.org. They take used furniture, a variety of household items (appliances, toys, dishes,

etc.), as well as cars, trucks, and RVs. They also have a "valuation guide" to give you an idea of the fair market value for the stuff you donate.

3. DRESS FOR SUCCESS: www.dressforsuccess.org. This is a terrific organization that gives business-type clothes to low-income women who are looking for jobs to support themselves and their families.

4. GLASS SLIPPER PROJECT: www.glassslipperproject.org. They accept formal wear, cosmetics, and accessories for needy Chicago high school students to wear to their proms. Links to similar organizations in other states are also posted.

5. BABY BUGGY: www.babybuggy.org. They're a nonprofit organization whose mission is to collect and redistribute infant gear and clothing to families in need.

EYEGLASSES

1. LIONS CLUB: www.lionsclub.org. Check out your local Lions Club online or drop 'em off at some of their affiliates, such as Lenscrafters, Sears, Pearle Vision, Sunglass Hut, and Target. They also take hearing aids.

2. NEW EYES FOR THE NEEDY: www.neweyesfortheneedy.com. Visit their Web site to learn how you can donate them. Used eyeglasses are given to folks in Third World countries while money from the sale of gold-filled glasses, hearing aids, and jewelry is used to buy new glasses for folks in the United States.

3. UNITE FOR SIGHT: www.uniteforsight.org. They accept your reading, distance, and nonprescription sunglasses and give them to children and adults in Nigeria, Malawi, Benin, Ghana, Uganda, Somalia, Cameroon, Congo, Guinea, Kenya, Tanzania, India, and Thailand.

TOYS, STUFFED ANIMALS, BOOKS, AND GAMES

1. CHILDREN'S AID SOCIETY: www.childrensaidsociety.org. They generally accept only new toys, clothes, books, and school supplies. But check with them since they may accept slightly used stuff if you bring it in for an evaluation.

2. TOYS FOR TOTS: www.toysfortots.org. They'll pick up the toys and distribute them to local campaigns throughout the country.

LOOSE CHANGE

1. HABITAT FOR HUMANITY: www.habitat.org. We all need a roof over our head, so whether you choose to pick up a hammer (watch your nails!) or write a check to them, you'll be helping those in need of housing around the world.

2. SUSAN G. KOMEN BREAST CANCER: www.komen.org. I think we're all familiar with this one, but it's so important to support all their efforts to find a cure as well as those of other cancer-fighting organizations, since breast, prostate, and skin cancer are touching so many.

3. THE ANGEL NETWORK: www.oprah.com. This is Oprah's baby and donations help fulfill The Angel Network's vision of helping women, families, and children around the world, whether it's by building or rebuilding (tsunami and Katrina), buying books or clothing, hiring teachers, or by giving to other charities. So be an angel and give!

4. TOMORROWS CHILDREN'S FUND: www.atcfkid.org. This is a privately funded, nonprofit organization that is dedicated to easing the pain and finding a cure for kids with cancer and blood disorders. It's a local fave of my son's and mine since we contributed "hands on" to it in years past by teaching kids to "cook up some fun." Their smiles said it all!

5. UNICEF: www.unicefusa.org. We all remember taking those cans

around at the holidays. Unicef collects money to help children worldwide be educated, clothed, and fed. The Red Cross is another tried-and-true option, too! Visit www.redcross.org.

Easy Rid Local Resources

Here are some quick and convenient local resources to "give" to:

- Food centers
- Libraries
- Houses of worship
- Hospitals
- Prisons
- Recreation centers
- Women's shelters
- Public schools
- Thrift shops
- Resale stores

AN ACCIDENTAL ASIDE

A Presidential Brief

If you see a turtle sitting on top of a fence post, it didn't get there by accident.

—BILL CLINTON

Let me preface this by stating that I think Bill Clinton is a brilliant guy. That said, what I'm about to share is done in the spirit of a good tale and not as an affront to his character. It seems that Bill and

Hillary were always "givers," and that before they moved into the White House they gave Bill's used underwear to The Salvation Army and listed it on their tax returns as a charitable deduction. Learning this made me feel good, since I have often and secretly given my old bras and undies away but never itemized them on our deduction list. But if our boy Bill can embrace the value of charity and line-by-line itemizing, why shouldn't an accidental housewife? Besides, giving is good for the soul and it's usually just a phone call away. Plus, if you have little ones, it's a great way to inspire and involve them in the art of giving versus receiving.

And, now it's truly Good Rid'ins 'cause you're done with this task!

TAKE FIVE AND ORGANIZE!

It's not too hard to get in the mood and maintain it if all you have is five minutes. So use it! Believe it or not, there are lots of things you can do to cut your clutter and get a little organized. Here are 15 of them:

1. Sort through mail.
2. Chuck junk mail.
3. Throw old magazines away.
4. Stack magazines you're keeping.
5. Edit kitchen countertop.
6. Fill dishwasher.
7. Empty garbage.
8. Clean junk drawer in kitchen.
9. Chuck expired meds in your bathroom cabinet.
10. Put toys into container.
11. Pay a bill or two.
12. Put shoes away.
13. Clear night tables.
14. Put jewelry away.
15. Call for pickup of stuff to give away.

TAKE-FIVE TASKS WANTED!

If you have any other ideas, please share them with all by visiting my website

www.theaccidentalhousewife.com.

Get Chi!

Jump for joy, you've gotten through another one of our acciden-tal housewifely activities and you're still smiling . . . I hope! If you're like me this was one tough task and I need to get chi. So pour yourself another cup of coffee or whatever else you're in the mood for and point it toward your mouth. Once again, fac-ing north is optional!

Take heart, the end is near!

Task #4
MEAL PLANNING & COOKING

FEEDING YOUR HOUSEHOLD WITHOUT REALLY TRYING!

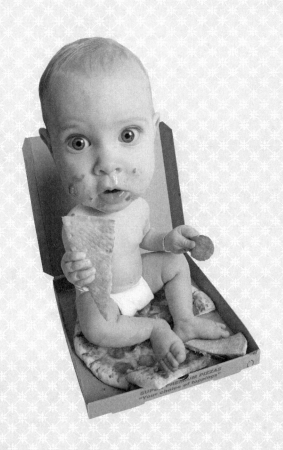

Mealtime: You may hate it, you may love it, you may have no time for it, or you may not be in the mood to make it, but you have to figure it out. Facts are facts—unlike cleaning, laundry, or organizing, which you can put off for weeks and even months without physical harm, you gotta eat, and the rule of thumb is that you should do it daily, preferably more than once. If you live alone or with another adult, this is fairly easy to do without much planning, but when you have multiple mouths to feed, it requires some thought, particularly if you want to control your urge to let them eat cake when they begin chanting: "I'm hungry—what's for dinner?" However, just as there are simple solutions for our other housewifely tasks, so there are for mealtime. They include buying in bulk, purchasing disposables, putting things in a designated place, and knowing which wines go with your mood. Sound familiar? It should, because these are the same types of things that you've learned can help with cleaning, laundry, and organizing. The circle is complete . . . let's eat!

THE ACCIDENTAL HOUSEWIFE'S MEALTIME BASICS

What my mother believed about cooking is that if you worked hard and prospered, someone else would do it for you.

—NORA EPHRON

Back in the 1950s a very smart guy named Gerry Thomas revolutionized mealtime cooking—he invented the famous Swanson TV dinner. Even back then, he realized that housewives were overwhelmed and would embrace anything that enabled them to fulfill any of their housewifely duties with little muss or fuss. All the better, too, if it gave them more time for themselves and they could watch Milton Berle or *The Honeymooners* on their favorite new TV. When you think about it, Gerry actually revolutionized the concept of ready-to-cook meals *and* disposable mealtime products—two things you'll use to feed your household without really trying. Of course, you may still have to defrost, reheat, or, if you choose, add your own personal touch, but like our ancestral housewifely species, you'll have more time for yourself and more time to watch *Oprah* or *Desperate Housewives* on your favorite new HI DEF TV. Don't you just love that guy!

Numero Uno Meal-Planning Rule: Fill 'Er Up! Pack Your Pantry and Fridge

Pretty simple advice here, but it will limit the time you spend worrying about feeding everyone every day and limit their complaints about having nothing around to eat. More good news: It doesn't require weekly shopping trips if you:

- POWER SHOP: Load up every two to three weeks (frequency determined by number of people in your abode and lifestyle).

- CYBER SHOP: If you're an online fan.
- SHOP SMART:
    - Buy a wide variety of foods to satisfy everyone's taste buds.
    - Purchase easy to prepare shelf-stable and frozen foods.

The Stuff You're Gonna Need

Before I suggest the key food categories you should focus on, it will be helpful for you to check out the places you currently use to store your food. As you do, ask yourself the following two questions:

- Can Your Freezer Hold a Cow? Got your attention! Is your freezer large enough to hold food to feed your family for at least two weeks? If you're single or have one other person in your household it should be; if three or more and you can afford it, consider buying a freezer the size of your tub. You'll thank me later. By the way, if you were thinking about buying a new fridge or are now that you've read this, go to the *Accidental Housewife's Buyer's Guide to Refrigerators* on page 127.
- Is Your Pantry Handy? By definition a pantry is a space designated for storing nonrefrigerated foods and wines. Unlike your bathroom, they aren't always obvious to identify since they can exist in a closet, a cabinet, or any space you choose. Just be sure it's large enough to hold what you need and it's close to the kitchen!

Your "Fill 'Er Up" Shopping List

In general your household's taste buds will guide your purchases, but having a clue as to what basics should go in there will simplify and reduce mealtime prep. This list is pretty broad and is divided into "necessities and excessities" for the pantry, the fridge, and the freezer.

Please note that *necessities* and *excessities* vary for each of us, so certain things may not be on the list. But the key is to load up so that anyone in your household will be able to whip up something they like anytime with little muss or fuss. A downloadable "Fill 'Er Up" Shopping List is available on my website at www.theaccidentalhousewife .com. It includes extra space for you to write in anything I forgot or any personal excessities!

THE FILL 'ER UP SHOPPING LIST

THE PANTRY

Please note: *Refrigerate after opening. **It's not absolutely necessary to refrigerate, but doing so will prolong the food's life. Just in case, check labels for any items you're not sure of.

Necessities:
- Olive oil
- Vinegar
  - Red
  - Balsamic
  - White
- Soy sauce
- Worcestershire sauce**
- Hot sauce
- BBQ sauce*
- Spaghetti sauce*
- Canned veggies*
- Canned soups*
- Canned tuna*
- Cereal
- Bread**

- Boxed starch:
  - Pasta
  - Potatoes
  - Rice
- Snacks:
  - Microwavable popcorn
  - Single-serving packs: chips, pretzels, popcorn, snack bars
- Salsa*
- Olives*
- Pickles*
- Coffee and/or tea
- Sugar
- Honey
- Maple syrup
- Jams and jellies*
- Peanut butter**
- Canned or bottled juices* (pineapple, cranberry, tomato, etc.)
- Soda*
- Shelf-stable Parmalat milk*
- Condiments: ketchup,** mustard,** mayo,* salad dressings*
- Herbs and seasonings of choice (Consider buying a fully stocked spice rack to simplify things.)
- Salt and pepper (FYI: I prefer kosher salt)

Excessities:
- Stuffed olives: perfect for martinis!*
- Cocktail onions*
- Beer*
- Wine*
- Cocktail mixers (Bloody Mary, daiquiri, piña colada, mohito, etc.)
- Espresso coffee
- Bottled water (with and without bubbles)

SERVING/PREPARING/STORING STUFF

Nonfood Necessities (pots, pans, and microwavable bowls optional):

- Napkins
- Paper towels
- Plastic utensils, plates, and cups
- Paper plates
- Freezer storage bags
- Microwavable cooking bags
- Aluminum cooking bags
- Aluminum foil
- Antibacterial kitchen soap
- Hand-sanitizing gel
- Cutting boards
- Digital-read food thermometer

Excessities:

- D.A. (See *The Accidental Housewife's Favorite Mealtime Tools* on page 150–51.)

THE FRIDGE

Necessities:

- Milk
- Eggs
- Cheeses (check out presliced varieties)
- Deli meats (check out presliced varieties)
- Fresh fruits
- Presliced and prewashed fresh veggies
- Meats, poultry, fish—only if using immediately

Excessities:

- Caviar
- Chilled wine or champagne

THE FREEZER

Necessities:

- Frozen, assorted:
  - Meats, poultry, fish—if uncertain when using
  - Precut veggies
  - Potatoes
  - Pizza
  - Fully cooked dinners
  - Breakfast faves: waffles, pancakes, bagels, egg sandwiches, bacon, etc.
  - Juices
- Ice cream or low-fat frozen yogurt
- Ice cubes

Excessities:

- Gourmet frozen appetizers
- Vodka
- Truffles (store in freezer and thaw overnight in fridge)

The Accidental Housewife's Buyer's Guide

REFRIGERATORS

If you're happy with the fridge that you have, move on. But if you're thinking your fridge is outdated, too small, or an eyesore, I've tapped the experts at Sears for some things to keep in mind as you look around. Per usual, I've included some personal things to help you pick the one best suited to your accidental needs and lifestyle. If you still want or need more info go to www.sears.com, click on "appliances," and check out their buyer's guide.

Here are a few things to think about:

- KITCHEN SPACE: Doors should be able to swing open fully, so measure first! Some models are lefty-friendly and come with reversible doors.
- SIZE/CAPACITY/NEED: Think about how many mouths you have to feed and room you need so you can fill 'er up!
- SPECIAL FEATURES:
  - Individual temp controls and humidity levels
  - Spill-proof glass shelves (easier to clean)
  - Adjustable door bins and shelves that also slide out
  - Self-defroster
  - Filtered-water dispenser
  - Energy and/or space-saving options:
    - In-door easy access refreshment center for beverages
    - On-door removable fruit and veggie basket to make washing stuff easier
    - Through-the-door ice and water dispenser
    - On-door removable ice caddy
    - Built-in wine rack
- DESIGN/COLOR/ATTRACTIVENESS/STYLE
- PRICE

Configure It Out!

As with everything else, leading appliance manufacturers such as Kenmore, Whirlpool, Maytag, and LG are always coming out with new options, energy-saving features, and designs. They also offer a variety of user-friendly configurations that you should explore. Keep in mind that most fridges extend beyond your counter, which is fine, but if you're willing to spend a little more you can purchase either a counter-depth fridge or a built-in.

Here are the styles to check out:

- SIDE BY SIDE: Fridge and freezer are side by side.
- BOTTOM MOUNT: Fridge on top and freezer below
- TOP MOUNT: Freezer on top and fridge below
- FRENCH DOOR: Fridge is full width of a side by side on top with freezer on bottom (great for big items).
- COMPACT: Mini version for dorms, supplementary usage, and key household drinking locales

Stuff You Wanna Know

I come from a family where gravy is considered a beverage.

—ERMA BOMBECK

Knowing the following may help you save time, money, and your sanity:

SHOP IN BULK

1. Stock up every two to four weeks with everything you need except freshness-sensitive items like milk, eggs, cheese, bread, veggies, fruit, and cut-to-order deli meats.

2. Buy multipacks of meat and poultry. When you get them home, split into individual meal servings and freeze. Also, buying multipacks may be cheaper, so check prices.

JOIN A PRICE CLUB

It's a jungle in there, but joining a price club like Costco, Sam's Club, or BJ's Wholesale Club can save you lots of money. On the flip side, a visit there can also cost you lots of money since there are so many food and nonfood temptations to buy, including things like a spanking-new plasma TV that's got your name and game on it!

In order to join a price club you usually have to pay an annual membership fee. Here are Web addresses for three of the more well-known clubs so you can learn more:

- Costco: www.costco.com
- Sam's Club: www.samsclub.com
- BJ's Wholesale Club (primarily in northeast): www.bjs.com

GRAZE WITH THE LOCALS

Sometimes, particularly on a nice weekend day, it's fun to visit your local farmer's market and pick up fresh foods and veggies. If the food part doesn't interest you, it's also a great people-watching activity and instead of food maybe you can "pick up" a date. Go to www.ams.usda .gov/farmersmarkets/map.htm to find the one nearest you.

GET HOME DELIVERY

Lots of the major supermarket chains and local markets offer home delivery and a huge assortment of ready-made, prepared meals. You can also find services online that deliver in your neighborhood, like FreshDirect, which is a local service in my area. The best way to find out who delivers in your area is to ask your local store or go online and Google home delivery services in your area. For those of you who don't know what Google is, it's a search engine. If you don't have Google, just go online and use whatever search engine you have. Use key words to localize it, like "NJ local supermarket delivery," or something close to that.

SIGN UP FOR A STORE CARD

Many local food chains offer their own savings card and the checkout cashier will usually swipe theirs if you forget yours. You've got noth-

WHAT'S YOUR MEALTIME HI Q?

What's Yukon Gold?

1. Dust spray
2. Cheap imitation gold
3. A potato
4. 1950s' TV show—famous gold-mining town
5. Hair color

How many teaspoons are in a tablespoon?

1. 2
2. 3
3. 4
4. 5

Which of the following is not a recommended way to thaw meat?

1. In cold water
2. In fridge
3. In microwave
4. On the counter

What does "al dente" mean?

1. You have a dent.
2. Firm against the teeth
3. Name of a famous Italian opera star
4. Let's get going

What is a tomato?

1. Fruit
2. Vegetable

ANSWERS: 3, 2, 4, 2, 1

ing to lose by having one and they generally cost nothing to sign up for, so it's a win-win.

COLLECT COUPONS

I'm not a coupon kinda gal. That takes some organization, which you learned some things about in the last chapter. But if you like clipping and saving you should, since it can save you some moola. Just put them where you can find them, perhaps in your wallet or on the door of your fridge, so you use them before they expire! Another option is to get your coupons online right before you go shopping so you don't have to go searching for them. Check out www.coolsavings.com—it offers lots of free money-saving coupons for food and other stuff. You can also go online and type in key words like "coupon savings in (your state)."

BUY NOW—FREEZE FOR LATER

Usually stores put large food items like turkeys, hams, and capons on sale right after the holidays. If you've got the room, fill 'er up for the future!

DON'T SHOP HUNGRY

If you go shopping and you're hungry, you're going to buy everything in sight either because it looks so yummy or you just want to blow out of there as quickly as possible. So eat first, shop later!

BUY PREWASHED AND PRECUT FRESH VEGGIES

This lets everyone eat or prepare stuff without any effort—an accidental housewife's perfect snack or side for yourself or anyone else!

INVEST IN DISPOSABLES

Why wash when you can toss! Think of disposable as your manicure-friendly way to cook, reheat, serve, freeze, and not wash dishes. There is a huge variety of disposable foil and microwave-safe cooking bags, meals that come in their very own microwavable containers, and attractive throwaway serving, cooking, and storage ware. What a wonderful world! See *The Accidental Housewife's Favorite Mealtime Tools* on page 150–51.

CHECK EXPIRATION DATES

Practically every food item has one, even soda, so be sure what you buy can stay around for a while without growing anything that can cause illness. Besides, your goal is to shop less often and items with short life expectancies will have you shopping more often. The following **Foodspeak** section will give you some helpful hints on this.

Foodspeak

Just like laundry has its own language for fabric care, so, too, has food and cooking, both in terms of how to prepare and of being able to decipher life expectancy. Unfortunately, unlike nutritional labels, expiration dates don't appear according to a standard system or in a standard location, and you may need a magnifying lens to read them and a GPS system to find them. But by knowing a few of the terms that follow, you'll be able to talk the talk and limit mealtime mishaps, illness, and/or starvation. FYI, common terms such as reheat, microwave, toast, or grill are not included. If you need these defined, it's best you refrain from cooking and eat out or hire a chef.

Menu of Terms

COLDSPEAK

- THAWING: One of the definitions I found defines it thusly: to change from a solid to a liquid through gradual warming; to become less aloof (have you ever met a steak that was aloof?). The proper way to "thaw" or defrost foods is in the fridge, cold water, or microwave according to package instructions. If you use the microwave, experts recommend cooking it immediately after thawing or putting the food back into the fridge for a limited time.

- DEFROSTING: The definition of defrosting is: to cause to thaw. So don't be confused if something says defrost or thaw—they're basically the same. Read thawing definition again for how to defrost!

BRAIN FREEZE

The Definition of Freezer Burn

I have always been fascinated how the words "freezer burn" can co-exist—they remind me of other equally odd word pairings like "jumbo shrimp," "head butt," or "living dead." Simply put, freezer burn occurs when frozen foods (particularly stuff like meats and ice cream) lose moisture or have been sitting in your freezer too long so that white or brownish spots, commonly referred to as "ice crystals," form. To prevent this from happening, it's good to date this kind of stuff before you freeze it so you'll know how long it's been sitting in there. Put the oldest stuff closest to the door, too, to help you mindlessly go for the oldest food first. By the way, if your meat is really, really brownish the food safety experts advise that you chuck it. If it's got just a little, it'll be OK if you scrape it off.

ICE CREAM TIP: To help prevent ice crystals from forming on your favorite flavor, put a piece of wax paper between the lid and the ice cream. I don't know why, but the experts say to do it, and I've found it works, so who am I to argue!

FRESHNESS SPEAK

The words in this section have been known to cause confusion, anger, and illness due to their variations and applications. My advice is to be aware of what they mean but to use your god-given senses to judge when food's gone around the bend: If it smells odd, you see stuff growing on it that doesn't look familiar, or its consistency has changed from a liquid to a blob—send it packing! It's not worth the risk. So what follows are my interpretations based on chatting with the pros, personal experience, and some hands-on research. You can also visit www.fsis.usda.gov for a more comprehensive food goodness guide.

- BEST BEFORE OR USE BY: This means how long it will stay fresh and retain its natural glow and quality. It's usually found on dairy items, freshly packed veggies, and refrigerated juices.
- PACKAGED ON: This lets you know when fresh food was packed and depending upon what it is, how long it's OK to eat. It's usually found on meats, cheeses, and presliced deli stuff.
- SELL BY AND SELL BEFORE: This indicates that the store knows to remove it from its shelves on a certain date. What's confusing with this one is that I've found that, in adjoining states, milk may have two dates: one for those living in the state where you live and another for the state next to yours. For example, my milk carton instructs: "Sell by April 15. In NYC sell by April 11." Does that mean if I buy it on April 12 and bring it to NYC it's no good? These are the things that boggle one's accidental mind!

  "Sell By" and "Sell Before" dates are usually found on milk and eggs. And if you weren't confused enough, eggs have one more dated instruction: "Use Before." Who's got this kinda time!! To know if your eggs are still worthy on or shortly after the "Use Before" date, check the *Eggs-tra! Eggs-tra!* box on page 136.
- BEST RESULTS IF USED BY: Are we thoroughly overwhelmed now? This phrase is often found on items such as refrigerated or frozen dough and refers to how long the ingredients are freshest and will perform at their best. I'm still at a loss to understand what "best" is, since I have often made cookies with dough that is well past its "best used" day and no visible or taste difference was apparent.

- FREEZE BY: If an item says this or if you freeze an item before its expiration date, you can ignore the date. Maybe we should just freeze everything! Well, maybe not everything. Stuff made from milk products can be frozen but milk will separate and can get grainy. Hard to semihard cheeses can be frozen and will taste OK, but they can become crumbly. Forget about cottage cheese and cream cheese. Now that I think about it, play it safe and just freeze that which you know can stand the cold, like ice cream!

- SHELF-STABLE: These are foods that you keep in your pantry and their life is not a question of food safety but of quality as it relates to taste, nutritional value, and texture. These include foods like cereals, pastas, rice, baking mixes, mustards, ketchup, and beans. Most of them will still have an expiration date, but shelf-stable stay fresher much longer.

EGGS-TRA! EGGS-TRA!

Freshness-Finder Cracked

For some reason, most of us forget how long eggs have been in our fridge and even when we check the "Sell By" and "Use Before" dates we still want to believe they have another few days of life in them. There is a way to know for sure and it's *really* easy—so easy that even your two-year-old can do it! Here's how:

- Fill a bowl with water and place (don't drop—remember, they're fragile!) one egg at a time into the bowl.
- If it sinks, you're good to go.
- If it swims, i.e., floats—it's going and so are you, as in going out for breakfast.

If only everything was this simple!

HEALTHSPEAK

When it comes to nutritional labels and terms, the key is to remember that they are *per serving*. So, if you have more than one serving, keep counting and paying attention. Here are a few common terms that you may choose to know and want to check:

- CALORIE-FREE: This means there are fewer than 5 calories.
- FAT-FREE: These are foods and drinks with less than ½ gram of fat per serving. If you have multiple servings it can start to add up since it doesn't say 0 fat. More disappointing news: Fat-free does not mean it is calorie-free or sodium-free, so you've got to read the rest of the fine print to find out.
- REDUCED-CALORIE AND REDUCED-FAT: This applies to foods and drinks with at least 25 percent less calories or fat than regular food.

THE DAILY GRIND

One of our favorite accidental indulgences is coffee, whether it's iced, latted, frapped, espressed, or straight up. So, for those of you who want or care to keep your java fresh, here's advice from the bean experts:

- Don't expose fresh coffee to air, light, heat, or moisture, since these will cause it to begin deteriorating.
- If unopened: Keep in freezer to maintain freshness for up to two months.
- If opened: Keep in cool, dark place like pantry. The fridge or freezer will cause it to lose freshness due to light and moisture.
- For best taste and to maintain freshness grind the beans as you use them.

- NO TRANS FATS: Trans fats are found in cooking oils, vegetable shortenings, some margarines, crackers, candies, cookies, snack foods, fried foods, baked goods, and other processed foods made with partially hydrogenated vegetable oils. They're the new bad boy, so food manufacturers are eager to point out when their products are free of them.

- LOW SODIUM: According to the experts, you shouldn't have more than 2,300 mgs of sodium a day. Sounds like a lot to me, but what do I know! Foods that say "low sodium" have less than 140 mgs per serving.

If you'd like to know more "healthspeak" check out my source: http://www.medicinenet.com/nutrition/article.htm.

Say Bye-Bye Bacteria

Support bacteria. They're the only culture some people have.

—UNKNOWN

Cook 'Em Out!

For those infrequent times when you or another in the household get the urge to acquaint yourselves with your oven or grill, it will be good to know how to safely cook your meats or poultry. Unfortunately, I like my meat rare, which I'm told is very unhealthy and probably means that my body is a condo unit for those little bacterial critters. If you want to avoid a similar situation take heed of the following tips and the Bye-Bye Bacteria Safe-Cooking Guide, which is provided courtesy of the NSF Center for Public Health Education.

- COOKING TIP: Recipes often tell you meat is done when the juices run clear. This refers to the color the liquid should be when you put a fork or knife into the center of the meat or poultry you're cooking. Anytime you see "red," unless you're a die-hard carnivore or angry, continue cooking. Pink's OK with beef, but clear and golden are best according to the experts!

- TEMP-TAKING TIPS: The first thing you'll want to get is a digital or instant-read food thermometer—your everyday household one won't do. When it comes to the big stuff like roasts and whole chickens and turkeys, you should use a large-dial thermometer. According to the pros you should always stick it into the thickest part of the meat, but *not* near the bone or in the fat. FYI: Temps shown are the recommended minimum internal heat. For more food safety tips go to www.nsfconsumer.org.

FYI: In drinks, "clear" refer to juices without pulp like white grape, apple, or pear juice, or to white wine, vodka, or gin.

SAYONARA SALMONELLA

No, this is not the Italian word for female salmon nor is it a condition caused by eating it. In fact, it has nothing to do with salmon. It is a bacteria that lives in animal feed and animals' intestines that can make you very sick if you don't cook your poultry, meat, or eggs thoroughly.

Maintain the Edge on Cutting Boards

Cutting boards are prime real estate for bacteria, so it's important to keep them clean. Here are some things to keep in mind:

- WOOD OR PLASTIC: It used to be conventional wisdom that wood cutting boards were a popular breeding haven for bacteria. But now lots of experts say wooden boards are less inviting to bacteria, since they're porous and deprive the little critters of water,

SAY BYE-BYE BACTERIA
Safe-Cooking Guide

Food Type	Recommended Internal Temperature
Poultry, whole (chicken, turkey) Thighs and wings (chicken, turkey) Duck and goose	180° F.
Poultry, breast only (chicken, turkey) Fresh beef (well done) Fresh pork (well done)	170° F.
Leftover meats Stuffing Ground meats (chicken, turkey)	165° F. JULIE'S TIP: Boil gravies
Ground meats (beef, pork, veal, ham) Pork, roast beef (medium) Ham (fresh) Eggs	160° F. JULIE'S TIP: Make sure yolks and whites are firm
Roast beef (rare) Fish	145° F. JULIE'S TIP: Fish should be opaque and flake easily with fork

SOURCE: NSF CENTER FOR PUBLIC HEALTH EDUCATION

http://www.nsf.org/consumer/food_safety/fsafety_cooking.asp?program=FoodSaf

which causes them to die. Plastic, on the other hand, lends itself to lots of nooks and crannies for them to set up shop. So, wood or plastic? It's your call.

- CLEAN OFTEN: Frequency is key: Use hot soapy water with a brush (don't forget your rubber gloves, too!), sanitize with distilled white vinegar. Pat dry with paper towels. Next time you're in the market for a new board buy one that's dishwasher safe. It doesn't have to be plastic since there are some dishwasher-safe wood boards. After cleaning, you can also rub a lemon over your wooden one to further squash those critters.
- BUY TWO: Use one board ONLY for raw meats, poultry, and fish. Use another *only* for fresh veggies, breads, and precooked stuff.
- CHUCK OLDIES: When you can't find a smooth section, it's time for that sucker to go packin'!
- OIL 'EM! Most of us probably won't do this, but it'll keep your wooden boards in better shape: Using a soft cloth, apply edible but tasteless oil every couple of weeks. It'll keep them from drying out and attracting bacteria. USP-grade mineral oil is recommended and it's the cheapest pure food oil you can buy. Olive or vegetable oil can turn bad, so save it for your salads and cooking.

TO 'WAVE OR NOT TO 'WAVE

No accidental housewifely home is complete without a microwave. The question becomes to 'wave or not to 'wave since even microwaves have their limits. What follows are some dos and don'ts to ensure you do as little as possible and that you don't hurt your best cooking bud, yourself, or the food you're 'waving.

NUMERO UNO DO!

ONLY USE CONTAINERS, LIDS, BOWLS, DISHES, BAGS, AND PLASTIC WRAP MARKED "MICROWAVABLE" OR "MICROWAVE SAFE"

Dos:

- Make sure foods and packages are microwavable. *Read instructions.*
- Defrost meats, fish, and poultry according to instructions.
- Microwave fresh veggies and fruits if you want to retain the most vitamins and minerals.
- Buy microwavable frozen foods that come in their own microwavable container or dish (less work for you!).
- Remember to cut a slit in the center of a microwavable bag so it doesn't explode.
- Uncover foods away from your face to avoid being burned by the escaping steam.
- Use microwave-safe white paper towels.
- Teach your kids how to use the microwave as soon as they learn how to use the remote so they can make their own meals.

NUMERO UNO DON'T!

NEVER PLACE METAL OR ALUMINUM FOIL IN MICROWAVE

Don'ts:

- Warm baby foods or formula in the microwave as there could be some dangerous hot spots. If you're stubborn or lazy and still want to use it, use the defrost cycle. Check and stir often. Always test the temperature before the feeding.
- Reheat in carry-out Chinese food containers—if metal handles are present.
- Melt butter or margarine in the plastic tub it comes in.
- Forget to use potholders to remove stuff.
- Reuse microwavable containers as they generally are meant for one use and can melt or fall apart.
- Use plastic storage bags that don't say they're microwavable, grocery bags, or newspapers.
- Dry your pet in it after bathing or being caught in the rain or a snowstorm.

INTERESTING TIDBIT

According to a study done at the University of Arizona, kitchens that look the cleanest are often the dirtiest since people who are always wiping their counters are spreading bacteria at the same time. Conversely, folks who never wipe counters, like single folks and particularly bachelors (sorry guys!), have cleaner kitchens. *So the moral of this study is...!*

THE MERITS OF MICROWARE

One of the most important things to have when using your microwave is what I refer to as microware. It's the right stuff to use when cooking, reheating, or defrosting. Fortunately, there are plenty of sizes and brands to choose from, and the best news is they're either disposable, dishwasher-friendly, or both. Here are a few well-known microware brands you should check out next time you're in the supermarket, at your favorite mass retailer, or online:

- GladWare containers and bowls: www.gladware.com
- Hefty Serve 'n Store Everyday Plates and Bowls: www.servenstore.com
- Ziploc Containers and Bags: www.ziploc.com
- Rubbermaid: www.rubbermaid.com
- Tupperware: www.tupperware.com

BURN THIS
Housewifely Calorie Counter

FEMALE: 125 lbs.

Moderately and continuously for 30 minutes

- Food shopping w/ cart: 65
- Unloading groceries: 71
- Eating (sitting): 43
- Eating (standing)*: 28
- Manicure (getting): 28

MALE: 165 lbs.

Moderately and continuously for 30 minutes

- Food shopping w/ cart: 86
- Unloading groceries: 94
- Eating (sitting): 56
- Eating (standing)*: 37
- Manicure (getting): 37

* Based on 15 minutes, since likelihood of you standing and eating longer than that is slim.

SOURCE: WWW.CALORIESPERHOUR.COM

CREATING MEALTIME MAGIC

The laziest man I ever met put popcorn in his pancakes so they would turn over by themselves.

—W. C. FIELDS

Now that you have a grip on the stuff you'll need and some general tips, it's time to perform some mindless mealtime magic for breakfast, lunch, and dinner. Breakfast and lunch ideas are kept to a minimum as those meals are usually eaten in a rush, on the run, or not at all. A few healthy food ideas that don't require any special talents are also included. But first, it's time again for a personal tale.

Opening Act: Breakfast

You're tired, you're cranky, and you haven't had your first cup of coffee. RULES ARE: If it can't be microwaved, put in toaster oven, or

AN ACCIDENTAL ASIDE

Cooking with Big Bird

I actually enjoy cooking, that is, when I have the time and I'm in the mood. In fact I used to cook several nights a week when my son ate baby food and my husband and I could dine at our leisure. But as my accidental housewifely life would have it, this luxury passed when my son's culinary desires were no longer satisfied by Gerber's best. A new strategy was required, and that strategy dawned on me as I watched him joyfully using the remote to navigate his way to Big Bird—Why not teach him how to cook! After all, if he could press a few buttons and add with Count Dracula, why not have him mash a few potatoes and press the minute button on our microwave? As it turned out, it was an act of genius! Now eleven and a member of the Culinary Institute (just kidding), he is my mealtime luxury, allowing me to cook when I have the time or I'm in the mood. Of course, not all of us have aspiring Emerils in our homes, but you may glean a clue watching how your child handles the remote and whether he or she is your built-in meal ticket!

doesn't come presliced or prepackaged, fuhgeddaboudit! Leave your house and go directly to McDonald's or your favorite bagel shop!

Serving Tips and Tricks:

- CEREAL: Purchase counter or wall-mountable food dispensers (love the ones found on www.zevro.com). They're great for portion control and self-serve. Fill with assorted cereals. Another option: buy single-serve, individually packed microwavable hot and cold cereal bowls.

- HOT STUFF: Buy an assortment of microwavable and/or toaster oven breakfast faves such as oatmeal, pancakes, waffles, bagels, bacon, egg sandwiches, etc.
- FRUITS: Bananas are often referred to as the perfect food. Buy a bunch. You can also purchase precut, canned, or packaged fruits. Pick those packed in their own juice vs. syrup—it's healthier.
- JUICE AND MILK: Buy and serve individual unsweetened juice packs or milk packs. There's even a shelf-stable milk called Parmalat, which my son loves since he thinks it tastes creamier.
- SERVE: If it doesn't come in its own container, use plastic or any other form of disposable tableware.

Putting Popcorn into Pancakes is Optional!

Act Two: Lunch

It's generally a luxury if you have the time to eat lunch out or peacefully pick through a salad at home. If it's just you, go to your neighborhood salad bar or corner hot dog vendor, or consider exercising instead of eating! But if you have kids, some lunchtime prep is required. RULES ARE: Buy presliced and prepackaged items and try to prepare the night before. Let your kids do as much age-appropriate stuff as possible. The more they're involved, the more likely they are to eat it, too.

FYI: The following are ideas for lunch that can be served at home or packed for you or your children, if you have them and there's no school cafeteria!

Serving Tips and Tricks:
- SANDWICHES: Roll up turkey, low-sodium ham, and/or cheese in a wrap with cranberry sauce, mustard, or low-fat mayo.

- FRUITS AND VEGGIES: Use precut and prewashed stuff including lettuce. Use disposables to pack them, like GladWare, Ziploc containers, or plastic bags. Buy individual salad dressing packages, yogurt tubes, or single-portion hummus packs for a veggie dip.
- SOUPS AND OTHER HOT STUFF: Check out all the tasty carry-and-go microwavable stuff like Campbell's Soup At Hand, Uncle Ben's Pasta Bowls or Rice (they claim on average they're 98 percent fat-free; however, I'm not sure of the rest of their nutritious splendor), and any other individually portioned stuff.
- SNACKS: Buy individually packed chips, pretzels or popcorn, granola bars, yogurt (kids love GoGurts!), presliced veggies and hummus, box of raisins, or indulge in a cookie or two—after all one should not live by healthy stuff alone!
- SERVE: Buy insulated lunchboxes or put ice packs in them. Use disposable sandwich bags, containers, and serving ware. For lunch box food-safety tips go to www.nsf.org.

TIP: If their lunch box has a nasty smell, soak a piece of bread in vinegar, place it in the box, and close it overnight. *Abracadabra!* the smell will be gone!

Final Act: Din-Din

I don't even butter my bread; I consider that cooking.

—KATHERINE CEBRIAN

Presto! Here's where we home in on your mealtime magic skills and truly embrace the art of feeding your family without really trying. It may take a little time to figure out just how to juggle your schedule, prep required, and dinnertime mood (See *The Accidental Housewife's Mood with Food Guide* on page 153), but you'll have the following bag of tricks to help you disappear sooner rather than later from the kitchen.

Serving Tips and Tricks:

- LET HONEY DO! Guys love to cook so long as the letters BB and Q are in the task. Obviously, it's a bit more challenging to BBQ if you live in an apartment or it's 10 below out, but thanks to the lovable George Foreman you can satisfy their or your love of grilling indoors. He's got lots of models, they come with tasty recipes, are pretty easy to clean, and because the fat drips down the food's a bit healthier. Visit www.esalton.com for George's latest and greatest. Also check out *The Accidental Housewife's Favorite Mealtime Tools* on page 150–51.
- MAKE MEALS THAT KEEP ON GIVING: On those rainy or snowy days when you've got some time and you're in the mood, consider cooking up some meals like turkey, meatloaf, stew, lasagna, or a Crock-Pot fave. The beauty of these dishes is that they generally yield leftovers and can be easily reheated, frozen, replated, or repurposed. Here's a quickie recipe that will keep on giving for days:

TEN-MINUTE TURKEY À LA J

This is one of my favorite recipes and meals because to prep the whole thing takes ten minutes, *and* I've got lots of leftovers. The key ingredient is the turkey, which you may be thinking is a pain to make since it takes forever to thaw or defrost (memories of FOOD-SPEAK!). Not anymore, if you buy my new best fowl cooking friend: Jennie-O. This bird has our accidental housewifely names on it: It comes in its own cooking bag, and requires *zero* thaw time. All you do is take it from your freezer, put it in the oven, and let it cook! *Love that!*

That leaves you about 9½ minutes to prep the rest!

- Microwave some frozen-fresh carrots and onions.
- Microwave frozen or boxed prepared potatoes or stuffing.
- Season veggies with a sprinkle of tarragon, salt, and a dab or two of butter.

If there's any leftover time, spend it opening, pouring, and leisurely gobbling down The Wine Chick's inexpensive pick: Estancia Pinot Noir ($10–12). Try to save some for din-din!

You can find some other tasty turkey recipe ideas at www.jennieo. com.

Ideas for the "final act" continues . . .

- Enlist the Military: The military learned years ago how to package foods that last and nowadays the meals have even gotten fairly tasty. They're real name is Meals Ready to Eat (MRE), so Google MRE or enter the words "military meals" to see what suits you and your household's buds.
- Multitask: Wash Your Dishes and Eat Fish, Too! Which brings me to my next personal tale:

AN ACCIDENTAL ASIDE

The Dish on Fish

One day my cousin Hope was over and I was sharing with her some of my mindless recipes. After I finished telling her about Ten-Minute Turkey à la J, she asked if I had ever tried poaching salmon in my dishwasher. At first I thought the wine we were drinking had gone to her head, but I responded with keen interest and a dash of doubt. But as an accidental housewife the idea of being able to cook and wash dishes at the same time was too good an idea to ignore, so I wrote down her recipe. I went to the store the next day and bought a few salmon fillets. When I got home, I washed them in the sink and placed them on heavy-duty foil. For seasonings I added a bit of butter, lemon, Dijon mustard, white wine, and garlic salt. I then sealed them in three layers of foil, fearful of leakage.

I put the salmon, now locked like Fort Knox, on the top tray of my dishwasher, sheepishly added my lemon detergent, closed the door, and started the wash cycle. Questions like: Would it be sudsy? Superb? Or would my dishes smell like salmon? swirled in my accidental mind.

GOOD NEWS: The salmon was perfectly cooked, my dishes sparkled, and the only bubbles I tasted were those of the champagne I served with the dish! I have since tried flounder, filet of sole, tilapia, and shrimp. The flounder and tilapia came out great. The shrimp turned out a bit mealy, but still tasty.

NOTE: The *Say Bye-Bye Bacteria Safe-Cooking Guide* on page 140 suggests that the internal temperature of safely cooked fish is 145°, so don't put your dishwasher on the economy or cold water cycle.

Now back to our tricks!

THE ACCIDENTAL HOUSEWIFE'S FAVORITE MEALTIME TOOLS

• HEFTY SERVE 'N STORE EVERYDAY PLATES AND BOWLS: You can heat up your food in the microwave, serve it, and even store leftovers on them. Every lid is a plate and every plate a lid . . . (let the villagers rejoice). They also have disposable cookware called EZ Ovenware casserole pans or EZ Foil aluminum pans. Check out www.servenstore.com for some simple recipes, too.

- TMIO: Now here's an oven that refrigerates your food before you're ready to cook it—an official "smart tool." And, you can do it all by calling in from your cell phone, going online, or setting it as an item on your honey-do list. It even has Sabbath settings. *Is this a great world or what!* Check it out for yourself at www.tmio.com. In case you're interested, TMIO stands for Today's Meal Interactive Oven.

- BEYOND MICROWAVE: This microwave comes with a bar code scanner and can read (and store) over 4,000 UPC codes from your favorite canned, frozen, or packaged foods. Give it a look at www.beyondconnectedhome.com. Yes, this too is a "smart tool." I think by now you see why these tools are called smart and why they're things you want to consider owning.

- GEORGE FOREMAN GRILL: He's a mean, lean grilling machine. You can't go wrong with any of his indoor grills. They keep introducing new and improved versions, so see what's the latest at www.esalton.com. It's also a mindlessly healthier way to grill since fat drips down and away from the food.

- PERFETTO PASTA COOKER: Pasta is the perfect meal and this product makes it quick and easy. Just boil some water in your teapot, pour into the cooker, add pasta, set your timer, and microwave some sauce. No bubbling over, no muss, no fuss—plus, it's dishwasher safe. Go to www.zevro.com for more info.

- TASSIMO HOT BEVERAGE SYSTEM: *This brew's for you!* I love this little baby. It will brew up something for everyone in your household one cup at a time. Get ready to enjoy a cup of coffee, tea, latte, milk-based cappuccino, espresso, or hot chocolate. What I love, too, is you can choose brewing pods from some of your favorite brands. Go to www.tassimo.com

- PEK WINE STEWARD: A must-have for any of us who have wasted good wine because we didn't want to get wasted! Now you can preserve that open bottle with little to no effort for weeks. Go to www.peksystems.com.

10 BEST NO-FUSS, FRESH, AND FILLING FOODS

1. **BANANA:** Peel and go.
2. **APPLE:** Wash and eat.
3. **CORN ON COB:** Husk and cook.
4. **BAKED POTATO:** Microwave or bake.
5. **CAMPBELL'S SOUP AT HAND:** Microwave and sip.
6. **HOT DOG:** Eat uncooked, broil, boil, or grill—pierce if putting in microwave.
7. **CHEESE:** Unwrap and munch.
8. **YOGURT:** Rip, then spoon or swallow.
9. **STAND 'N STUFF TACOS:** Stuff with whatever, including precooked (and preprepped) beef, chicken, or deli meats and cheeses.
10. **REFRIGERATED COOKIE DOUGH:** Slice and bake.

• GET M.O.M. ON THE LINE: Delivery and take-out foods from your favorite local places are easy and convenient, but if you're looking for something that your local guys might not offer, there are a few M.O.M. (Mail Order Meals) available online or in catalogs to tempt your palate. They may cost a little more because of shipping or their "gourmet" quality, but they're worth indulging in occasionally and you can freeze them.

Here's my 411 on a few I've tried:
- Deep-Dish Pizza: www.deepdishpizza.com
- Ribs and all the Fixin's: www.shopstickyfinger.com
- Beef, Chicken, Meatballs, Stew, Ravioli—EVERYTHING: www.alazing.com
- Surf and Turf: www.omahasteaks.com
- Gourmet Meals from some of America's most prestigious

chefs: Daniel Boulud, Mark Miller, and Charlie Trotter: www.fiveleaf.com

  • Coconut Cake to die for! www.peninsulagrill.com

• PUT FAVORITE TAKE-OUT PLACES ON SPEED DIAL. Self-explanatory, I hope!

FEEDING FIDO WITHOUT TRYING

Like the other members in your household, your pets need their daily serv-ings of food and water. Here are a few products that are available online at petsmart.com and amazon.com that can help them avoid starvation or thirst without you really trying! FYI: If neither of these sources has them, just search by name online or call your local pet shop.

• Le Bistro Automatic Waterers and Feeders
• Blitz Feeder and Watering System
• PetZazz Self-Feeding Dispensers
• Ergo Automatic Waterers and Feeders
• PetSafe 5-Day Feeder
• Catit Drinking Fountain

  Alternatively:

• Buy a stuffed toy animal or a robotic pet.

THE ACCIDENTAL HOUSEWIFE'S MOOD WITH FOOD GUIDE

Women complain about PMS, but I think of it as the only time of the month when I can be myself.

—ROSEANNE BARR

You've now got enough mealtime tricks, tips, and sources to keep you and your household from starvation. What you're missing is something just for you! That's where the handy dandy Mood with Food Guide comes in. It's your answer to matching your mood du jour with what your body's craving, the right varietal (courtesy of the Wine Chick), or what you're in the mood to do or not do at dinnertime— either for yourself or others. I've included brief mood descriptions just in case you can't put your finger on whether you're feeling manic, sweet, selfish, or lazy, or just need an excuse to indulge.

Mood with Food Guide

Bitch-of-a-Day Mood

You didn't get the raise you hoped for, your car broke down, your baby wouldn't nap, you ruined your new shoes in the rain, or you noticed you're losing your hair. You need some TLC and fast-acting over-the-counter pain relievers.

FOOD

Eat comfort foods that remind you of gentler, kinder days when Mom cooked (maybe!): mashed potatoes, meatloaf, southern fried chicken, and apple pie. Good idea to stay away from sharp objects when preparing these foods due to the mood you're in.

VARIETAL

You probably want to grab what's open or nearby, but if you have the time to think about or prepare ahead, go for a big, bold Chardonnay. Two to consider are a moderately priced one from Toasted Head ($10–$15) and a bit more indulgent one from Sonoma Cutrer ($18–$22). These wines have a higher alcohol content that will help to intensify and expedite the effect of a glass—a perfect complement for this kind of day and mood.

Let-'Em-Eat-Cake Mood

You're feeling overextended, your mother's complaining you don't see her enough, or your significant other is out with friends—thus you could care less if others starve since no one seems to care about you.

FOOD

Let them eat frozen meals, takeout, cold leftovers, cake, or eat out— anything that doesn't require your being involved or nearby.

VARIETAL

Shut your bathroom door, run that bubble bath, and pour yourself a soft, pearlike Pinot Gris Trimbach ($9–$12). It will help take you even farther away from those eating cake.

PMS Moods

Moods is the operative word here, since you vacillate from feeling sad, bloated, fat, tired, hateful, ready to kill anyone who gets in your way, to weepy, sentimental, and oversensitive.

FOOD

Anything fattening, high in grease (fried Mexican and Italian foods are great PMS elixirs), sweet (half gallons of ice cream, chocolate), and lots of wine or other mood-elevating substance. If you're like me you'll crave a side of beef. TIP: Don't schedule a cholesterol test near this time of the month. See Pig-Out foods, too.

VARIETAL

The Wine Chick says there's only one option that truly works with PMS, and she bases this both on her expertise and on personal PMS bouts: Sandeman 10-year-old Tawny Port ($25–$30). It's got all those rich tastes you're craving, so you won't have to dive into a piece of cherry chocolate cheesecake—at least not while drinking your first glass! Plus it's higher in alcohol, so it'll help relieve those cramps! FYI: Though it's a little pricey, it'll provide several months' worth of PMS relief since it is meant to be savored in moderation and not consumed in one seating.

Love-Is-Grand Mood

Ahh, that queasy easy feeling of being in love and feeling as though the world is a magical place. Hold on to it for as long as you can, not only because of the way it makes you feel, but because it frequently causes weight loss, since love, not food, is on your mind.

FOOD

Anything indulgent and/or a natural aphrodisiac like chocolate, bananas, strawberries, and oysters.

VARIETAL

Since love is grand and you're mind's off in la-la land, just splurge. Indulge in a bubbly from the guys who grew the original grape on champagne—the French (my fave): Tattinger La France ($35–$40).

Over-the-Sink Mood

You've gotten home late from work, didn't eat your dinner since you were too busy drinking and yakking, you're too lazy, you drank too much, and/or just want to eat without muss or fuss.

By the way, there's a name for people like you: sinkies. You've got an association and a Web site you should visit: www.sinkie.com. I recommend you do that *after* you finish eating over the sink.

FOOD

Leftovers are best, particularly Chinese in their boxes; anything you can eat directly from their source: ready-made soups and frozen meals in their own serving container; peanut butter off the spoon; milk out of the carton with cake or cookies; and/or ice cream out of the container.

VARIETAL

Any single-serving wine cooler will do, or if you want something with a little more pizzazz, grab a can of Sofia Mini Blanc de Blanc Sparkling Wine (it's named after Francis Ford Coppola's daughter). You can buy it individually for $5 or in a four-pack for $20.

Pig-Out Mood

You're feeling lonely, your clothes are too tight, you just broke up with your significant other, you're PMSing, and/or you're trying to quit smoking.

FOOD

Eaten in quantity: chips, fries, fast food, greasy stuff, Chinese takeout, Jewish deli sandwiches, pizza with the works, cookies, ice cream, chocolate, and anything else that isn't an individual serving. Also check Bitch-of-a-Day Mood and PMS Moods warning. Be prepared tomorrow for a PMS or Let-'Em-Eat-Cake Mood since you'll be feeling fat and therefore bitchy or bastardly.

VARIETALS

Go with a Coastal Ridge Pinot Grigio ($6–$8). It's light, fresh, and sweet, so it will go with anything you're chowing down. And it's cheap, which is perfect given the junk quality of the food you're consuming! *Alternatively:* Pig out with a six-pack of your favorite beer!

Martha Mood

Rare, but these kinds of moods can happen. You're feeling perky, ambitious, just watched The Food Network, and want to experience the joys of cooking. The key is to keep the feeling and your enthusiasm going long enough to finish preparing the meal. You can do this by preparing recipes that aren't too complicated, but will garner lots of compliments and leftovers—both "good things" since the odds are that in an hour or tomorrow your Martha Mood will pass and your Let-'Em-Eat-Cake Mood will return.

To help you, I've included one of my favorite recipes that has pacified my Martha moments on many occasions—it's also a great dish for company. It's called Duck à la Edie: named after my mother, who was a very good cook but has boarded her kitchen up after discovering dining out beats cooking—*Go Mom!* Let me know how you and yours like it! Some sample sides and a tasty varietal to accompany Duckie follows this recipe.

DUCK À LA EDIE

Serves 2
(Double for four, triple for six and so on.)

One whole duck, cleaned by others (approximately 5–6 lbs.)
Salt and pepper to taste (I like kosher salt, but it's your call.)
1 12 oz. can frozen orange juice (no pulp)
1 10–12 oz. jar of red currant jelly
¼ cup Grand Marnier (or more to taste)

1. Preheat oven to 375°F.
2. Salt and pepper duck to taste.
3. Put whole duckie on rack in a disposable cooking pan so fat drips.
4. Pierce duck with a fork frequently while cooking to let fat out.

5. Prepare sauce in small saucepan: Add frozen OJ. Turn burner on moderate and let OJ melt completely. Stir in currant jelly with OJ and blend well. Mix in Grand Marnier and continuing blending over low heat.

6. Cook duck for about 1½ hours or until skin is nice and crispy. (Recommended internal temp is 145°F. I usually know it's done when thigh easily separates and the duck's no longer quacking. *Just Kidding!* Don't worry about overcooking, since you really can't do that to duck unless you burn it.)

7. Let cool.

8. Use cooking shears to cut duck into pieces (legs, thighs, breasts, etc.).

9. Pour out grease,

10. Wash out disposable pan or use a new one.

11. Place duck into pan and coat evenly with sauce on both sides. Save some sauce for serving.

12. Put under broil for approximately 25 minutes. Turn often and let each side get crispy. Feel free to put a bit more sauce on.

Serve from Duckie's cooking container or on a platter (disposable's fine!) with the simple sides and varietal.

Simple Sides:

Microwave a precooked rice dish like Uncle Ben's Wild Rice and a veggie like frozen-fresh Brussels sprouts. Embellish Brussels sprouts with butter and garlic. If you're feeling a bit more indulgent, add a teaspoon of truffle oil to the sprouts and toss gently.

VARIETAL

Norman Old Vine Shiraz ($15–$20) or BR Cohn Carneros Chardonnay ($20–$25). Either choice will help you continue your fleeting masquerade as a chef with pizzazz and wine know-how!

Congratulations!!!
You Are Outta Here!

Way to go, fellow accidental housewives! You've made it through your final task and hopefully found that coming out of the broom closet and admitting to your fear, loathing, disinterest, or imperfection can be embraced with a smile and overcome fairly easily with the right stuff. Now, just as you started this book, grab your favorite libation and get the two of you outta here! Future tasks await us, but that's stuff for another day. Here's to our species . . . *we rock!*

About the Author

JULIE EDELMAN is a well-known lifestyle reporter who regularly shares her accidental housewifely wit and wisdom on ABC's *The View* and has appeared on CBS's *The Early Show,* NBC's *Early Today,* WB, Fox, and The Food Network as well as on a variety of national and local radio shows. Julie contributes to and has been featured or quoted in several magazines including *First for Women, Parenting, Good Housekeeping, Time, New Jersey Monthly,* and Scholastic's *Parent & Child.* Julie hosts theaccidentalhousewife.com and is an expert contributor for ClubMom.com, YourLifeMagazine.com, and Beststuff.com. She celebrates our fear, loathing, or disinterest in housewifely life in live, fun-filled, sanity-saving public appearances.

Before coming out of her broom closet and admitting to her accidental ways, Julie was a senior VP at Bohbot Entertainment; senior VP/creative director at Saatchi and Saatchi Advertising, and wrote a children's cookbook, *Once Upon a Recipe* (which she claims turned out to be a stroke of genius since it got her son into cooking and now she doesn't have to!)

She is pursuing a life-long degree from the not yet accredited Accidental Housewifely School of Living Arts to complement her formal degree from Duke University. All free time she has left is spent living life to its accidental housewifely fullest with her family and dog, Woody, in New Jersey.